Dhruvil Patel

INDIA · SINGAPORE · MALAYSIA

Copyright © Patel Dhruvil Dharmendra 2024
All Rights Reserved.

ISBN 979-8-89446-066-6

This book has been published with all efforts taken to make the material error-free after the consent of the author. However, the author and the publisher do not assume and hereby disclaim any liability to any party for any loss, damage, or disruption caused by errors or omissions, whether such errors or omissions result from negligence, accident, or any other cause.

While every effort has been made to avoid any mistake or omission, this publication is being sold on the condition and understanding that neither the author nor the publishers or printers would be liable in any manner to any person by reason of any mistake or omission in this publication or for any action taken or omitted to be taken or advice rendered or accepted on the basis of this work. For any defect in printing or binding the publishers will be liable only to replace the defective copy by another copy of this work then available.

A lot can happen before December 31.

Trust God

Contents

ROAD MAP

1: Breaking the Chains

1. What is the "matrix" and how does it limit us?
2. Why do we need to break free from the matrix?
3. How can we break free from the matrix?
4. What are some examples of people who have broken free from the matrix?
5. How can we develop the mindset of freedom?

2: The Power of Mindset

1. What is a growth mindset and why is it important?
2. How can I develop a growth mindset?
3. What are limiting beliefs and how do they affect me?
4. What is visualization and why is it useful?
5. How can I practice visualization?

3: Money Matters

1. What is financial literacy and why is it essential for achieving financial freedom?
2. Why is investing in yourself and your skills crucial for achieving financial freedom?

3. How can we manage debt effectively and avoid falling into the debt trap?

4: Hustle and Grit

1. What are side hustles and how can they contribute to financial freedom?
2. How can we identify and pursue side hustles that align with our passions and skills?
3. How can we embrace failure and learn from setbacks in our side hustle endeavors?
4. What are the key characteristics of a successful side hustle entrepreneur?
5. How can we balance our side hustles with our personal and professional lives?

5: Digital Age Opportunities

1. How can the digital age empower individuals to pursue their passions and build fulfilling careers?
2. How can the digital age enhance financial literacy and empower individuals to make informed financial decisions?
3. How can entrepreneurs harness the power of digital technology to launch and grow their businesses?
4. How can the digital age empower individuals to contribute to social impact and global change?
5. How can the digital age facilitate lifelong learning and personal growth?

6. How can the digital age promote global collaboration and cross-cultural understanding?
7. How can the digital age enhance access to information and knowledge for individuals worldwide?
8. How can the digital age foster innovation and entrepreneurship in developing countries?

6: Networking and Mentorship

1. Why is networking important for young people seeking financial independence?
2. How can young people identify and connect with potential mentors?
3. What are some key qualities to look for in a mentor?
4. How can young people make the most of their mentorship relationships?

7: Escaping the Rat Race

1. What is the rat race, and how does it limit financial freedom?
2. How can one redefine financial independence beyond material gains?
3. What are some alternative paths to financial freedom besides the traditional 9-to-5 career?
4. How can one adopt a growth mindset to embrace continuous learning and adaptability?

5. What are some practical steps one can take to start their journey towards financial freedom?

8: Health Is Wealth

1. Why is prioritizing health essential for achieving financial independence?
2. What are some practical steps to maintain physical and mental health on a tight budget?
3. How can maintaining a healthy work-life balance contribute to achieving financial independence?
4. How can mindfulness and meditation practices enhance your financial decision-making?
5. How can prioritizing sleep contribute to your financial success?
6. How can creating a supportive network of friends and family contribute to your financial success?
7. How can actively seeking guidance from financial professionals enhance your financial independence journey?

9: Legacy and Impact

1. Why is leaving a positive legacy important when pursuing financial independence?
2. How can defining your personal values and beliefs guide your philanthropic endeavors?
3. How can you effectively identify and support organizations that align with your philanthropic goals?

4. How can you balance your financial goals and aspirations with your philanthropic endeavors?
5. What are some creative ways to make a positive impact beyond traditional monetary donations?
6. How can you inspire and empower others to pursue their own philanthropic endeavors?
7. How can you effectively communicate your philanthropic endeavors to others?
8. How can you ensure that your philanthropic legacy extends beyond your lifetime?

10: Your Journey Begins

1. How can you overcome procrastination and take action towards your financial goals?
2. How can you craft a personal manifesto that encapsulates your financial goals, values, and aspirations?
3. How can you become a catalyst for change and inspire the youth revolution?
4. How can you balance pursuing your financial goals with living a fulfilling and purposeful life?
5. How can you overcome limiting beliefs and negative self-talk that may hinder your financial progres
6. How can you leverage technology and innovation to enhance your financial success?

7. How can you cultivate a mindset of abundance and resilience in the face of setbacks and challenges?
8. How can you build a strong financial foundation and protect your financial well-being?
9. How can you contribute to a more equitable and sustainable financial future for all?
10. How can you overcome the fear of failure and embrace the spirit of risk-taking in your financial endeavors?
11. How can you maintain a healthy and balanced lifestyle while pursuing your financial goals?
12. How can you harness the power of gratitude and cultivate a spirit of abundance to transform your financial future and achieve your ultimate financial goals?

1

BREAKING THE CHAINS

What is the "matrix" and how does it limit us?

When we talk about the "matrix," we're basically diving into the invisible playbook of rules, norms, and society's expectations that shape our lives. It's like this secret force molding our thoughts, values, and every move we make. Think of it as the puppet master pulling the strings behind the scenes, directing our actions, shaping our thoughts, and even playing a role in our personalities. It's the shadowy origin of a bunch of fears, doubts, and those pesky insecurities we all wrestle with.

The matrix is not inherently bad or evil. It is the result of human history, culture, and evolution. Its purpose is to maintain social order, stability, and harmony. It promotes cooperation, communication, and coexistence with others.

Now, let's chat about the matrix's quirks. It's not all rainbows and butterflies; there are a few glitches. Imagine it as a creativity clipper, an individuality smoother, and a freedom fence. Sometimes, it throws roadblocks on the path to our passions, dreams, and goals, boxing us into a cycle of same old, same old - the land of conformity, mediocrity, and a dash of dissatisfaction.

Think of the matrix as a cosmic fingerprint - it's not a one-size-fits-all deal. It's like a shape-shifter, morphing based on where we come from, the vibe around us, and the cards life deals us. There are those who cozy up to it, feeling like it's their comfort zone, while others might sense a bit of alienation and oppression in the mix. And then, there's this awareness spectrum; some folks are like matrix whisperers, fully tuned in, while others navigate through life with a blissful lack of matrix radar. It's like a cosmic dance where everyone has their unique rhythm.

The matrix isn't set in stone; it changes as our society moves forward. It's not this rigid, unchanging thing. If you're open to thinking, acting, and being different, you can question it, challenge it, and even transform it. It's not this permanent fixture - it's more like a fluid thing that moves with the times.

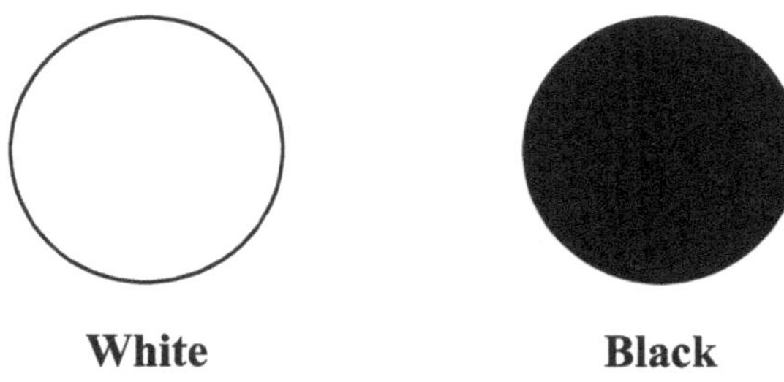

White **Black**

Of the two circles given to you one circle is larger than other,

Choose any one,

- ☐ **White**
- ☐ **Black**

Maybe you choose white one or

Maybe you choose black one.

But Now I am saying those two circles are same.

What was you learned?

You made your mind according to the information, which was I given.

But Worst part of thinking there were two circles in front of you, clear result in front of you.

You have eye to see truth but the matrix wants to show you what it wants.

Why do we need to break free from the matrix?

Breaking free from the matrix entails freeing ourselves from the limitations and constraints that society places on us. It entails taking control of our own lives, making our own choices, and charting our own course. It means living authentically, passionately, and purposefully.

Getting out of the matrix isn't a walk in the park. It takes guts, a strong will, and the ability to bounce back when things get tough. It's not a straightforward journey; there are risks, uncertainties, and sacrifices involved. Plus, breaking free might stir up some conflict, face pushback from others, and even trigger our own fears, doubts, and guilt.

Yet, the journey of breaking free from the matrix is incredibly rewarding and fulfilling. It opens doors to growth, learning, and exciting discoveries. Opportunities and possibilities unfold, showcasing your true potential. The process itself brings joy, happiness, and a sense of satisfaction. Moreover, it becomes a source of inspiration, empowerment, and influence for not just yourself but others as well.

Escaping the matrix isn't a one-shot deal or a spot on a map where you plant your flag. It's more like an ever-flowing river, a lifelong adventure. It's not a task you tick off but a daily dance, a series of moments, and a cascade of choices. It's the art of unfurling your wings every day, painting your own canvas in each moment, and weaving the tapestry of your journey with every choice, like a storyteller crafting a never-ending tale.

How can we break free from the matrix?

Breaking out of the matrix is like embarking on a personalized cosmic quest—no one-size-fits-all manual here. Picture it like a buffet of liberation, where each person gets to craft their unique escape route, sculpted by their own situation, dreams, and flavors of preference. Yet, in this wild journey, there are some shared steps, like hidden treasures on the path, that can guide us through the matrix maze and unlock the door to our own bespoke freedom.

First things first: we need to be aware of the matrix. It's like opening our eyes to the behind-the-scenes puppetry in our lives. Look around and notice the unspoken rules, society's expectations, and all those norms we're supposed to follow. Now, think of it as giving these norms a little side-eye. It's time to question and challenge the .beliefs and values we've picked up along the way. Imagine it as taking a step back and saying, "Wait, do I really want to dance to this tune?"

Let's groove into the second step: crafting a freedom mindset. It's like tending to your mental and emotional garden, planting the seeds that'll sprout your escape from the matrix. Picture it as flexing your mental muscles, cultivating a growth mindset that whispers, "Hey, I can learn, evolve, and shake things up!" Next, kick out those party-crashers known as limiting beliefs – those sneaky, negative thoughts about ourselves, others, and the big wide world. Imagine it's like giving them a swift boot and reclaiming your mental space. Lastly, let's sprinkle in some starry-eyed magic – visualizing success. It's about conjuring up your dream future in your mind's eye, creating a mental masterpiece of the life you want.

Step three is all about making moves toward freedom: It's not just a mind game – we're talking practical actions here. Think of it like putting on your action-hero cape in the real world. First up, sketch out a plan. This isn't some complex blueprint; it's more like a friendly guide nudging you towards your goals. Next, dive into what makes your heart sing – find and chase your passion. That's like doing the things you love and enjoy, making life a bit more colorful. Now, let's tackle the F-word – failure. Instead of fearing it, see it as a chance to learn and step up your game. Lastly, channel your inner superhero with persistence. It's about-facing hurdles head-on, keeping at it, and showing those obstacles who's boss.

Now, let's dive into step four: where we tap into the magic of the digital realm. It's like unleashing the superheroes of technology to aid our quest. Imagine this as a futuristic treasure hunt where we harness the tools and resources that the digital age generously hands us. Picture yourself as an explorer, venturing into the vast landscapes of e-commerce, blogging, podcasting, and all those online adventures. Think of freelancing and gig economy as your trusty sidekicks, offering flexibility, autonomy, and a colorful array of opportunities. Now, here's the fun part – crafting and growing your digital alter-ego, your personal brand. It's like painting a vibrant mural of your reputation and image in the online world.

Let's step into the fifth gear of our Matrix escape journey: the art of connecting and collaborating. Imagine it as not just building connections but crafting a cosmic alliance to fuel your quest. Mentors become your mystical guides, the Gandalfs and Yodas who've conquered the challenges you're facing and are ready to share their wisdom. Now, envision communities as your fellowship, a diverse group of kindred spirits who share your interests, values, and cosmic goals. It's not just joining – it's actively contributing to this magical circle. Finally, think of feedback as the secret language of growth – a magical scroll passed among fellow travelers, sharing insights, advice, and the alchemy of improvement to help everyone evolve on this epic escape from the Matrix.

The sixth step is to design and craft our lifestyle: the art of lifestyle design. It's like picking up the cosmic paintbrush and sketching out the life canvas that truly vibes with you. Imagine this as your personal masterpiece, where you get to decide the hues and strokes. Corporate or entrepreneurship – think of it as choosing between different realms of work and income, each with its own magical charm. Now, let's add a touch of flair – your personal style. It's not just about clothes; it's the way you talk, the way you move, the essence of your cosmic groove. Lastly, let's sprinkle in some financial magic – achieving and maintaining independence. Picture it like having your own treasure chest, enough cosmic coins to sail through life without being tethered to the daily grind.

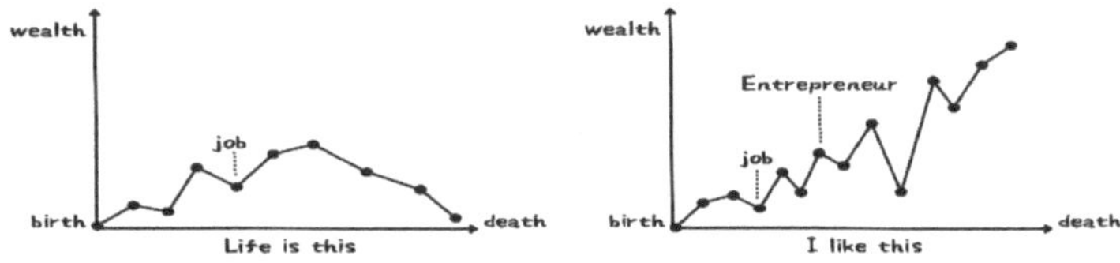

Welcome to the seventh realm of our Matrix escape: the sanctuary of health and well-being. Picture it as crafting your personal temple, where your mind and body dance in cosmic harmony. Now, let's add a dash of magic – it's not just about health; it's a celebration of vitality. Think of it like planting a garden of well-being where you nourish your body with good eats, dance with the stars through regular exercise, and tuck yourself into cosmic slumber every night. Next up, the stress-busting ritual – it's like conjuring spells to banish the pressure and tension that life throws at you. Lastly, mindfulness – think of it as sipping on the elixir of awareness and attention, soaking up every moment in this grand cosmic spectacle.

Welcome to the eighth and final act of our Matrix escape: the legacy chapter, where we etch our cosmic mark on the universe. Imagine it as crafting a celestial story with purpose and meaning, a narrative that reverberates through the cosmic echoes. Now, let's add a touch of stardust – it's not just about living; it's about showering the world with your unique gifts, talents, and skills. Picture it as a cosmic performance, where you take center stage and share the magic only you possess.

Next up, the impact dance – it's about making waves, creating ripples of positivity for others and the very fabric of the environment. Lastly, the inspiration magic – think of it as becoming the cosmic muse, urging and empowering others to join the dance of breaking free from the matrix and living their most extraordinary lives.

What are some examples of people who have broken free from the matrix?

Well, let me tell you, there's a whole constellation of them out there, shining in different ways and fields. Some might be familiar faces you've seen in the spotlight, while others prefer to dance in the shadows, quietly savoring their freedom. Imagine a cosmic gallery showcasing individuals who've not just achieved financial freedom but also soaked up the sweet nectar of personal fulfillment. It's like a diverse tapestry where each thread tells a unique story of escape and triumph.

Let me introduce you to some cosmic trailblazers who've orchestrated their own escape from the matrix and are now painting the universe with their unique strokes:

Tim Ferriss: Ever heard of the guy who wrote the blueprint for breaking free from the 9-to-5 grind? Tim's the maestro behind "The 4-Hour Workweek," and he's not just an author; he's a podcasting, entrepreneurial, investing, lifestyle-designing wizard. From mastering languages to cooking up a storm, Tim's the jack of all cosmic trades.

Oprah Winfrey: A cosmic luminary, Oprah has lit up the media galaxy like no other. The queen of talk shows, she's not just a host but a producer, philanthropist, and the guiding force behind an influential book club. Rising from a challenging past, she's now a billionaire and a beacon of inspiration for many.

Elon Musk: Ever dreamt of making humanity a multi-planetary species? Elon's your guy. The brains behind Tesla, SpaceX, and Neuralink, he's the pioneer navigating the cosmic frontiers of electric vehicles, space exploration, and brain-computer interfaces. His mission? To solve the world's most gigantic puzzles.

Marie Forleo: Meet the cosmic mentor on MarieTV, an online show sprinkling wisdom for entrepreneurs and creatives. She's also the mastermind behind B-School, an online business school shaping dreamers into doers. A motivational force with the mantra "everything is figureoutable," Marie envisions a world where everyone uses their gifts to change the cosmic narrative.

Gary Vaynerchuk: In the realms of media and communications, Gary's the cosmic commander-in-chief. As the brains behind VaynerX and VaynerMedia, he's a digital sage working with global brands. Beyond business, he's an entrepreneur, investor, author, and speaker. With a goal of owning the New York Jets, his cosmic message is all about "crushing it" in both life and business.

How can we develop the mindset of freedom?

Alright, imagine the mindset of freedom as your magical key to unlocking the cosmic gates of escape from the matrix. It's not just a mental state; it's a dynamic attitude and perspective that empowers us to dance to our own rhythm – independently, creatively, and with a splash of confidence. Think of it as the bedrock, the heartbeat of our power and untapped potential, echoing through the cosmic corridors of our journey.

Picture the mindset of freedom as a cosmic art form – it's not bestowed upon us at birth like a celestial gift. Instead, it's this ever-evolving skill, a dance we can learn, polish, and perfect. Think of it as a symphony we practice and eventually master, a habit we carefully nurture and keep alive.

Now, let's imagine this cosmic dojo where we sharpen the mindset of freedom. It's not a one-size-fits-all journey; it's more like a buffet of strategies waiting for you to taste and savor. These are the cosmic ingredients that can sculpt and mold your mindset into a masterpiece. Read books and articles that inspire and educate you about the mindset of freedom. Some of the recommended books are the 4-Hour Workweek by Tim Ferriss, Rich Dad Poor Dad by

Some other books that can help you develop the mindset of freedom are:

- **The Power of Now by Eckhart Tolle** - which teaches how to live in the present moment and free yourself from the past and the future.

- **The 7 Habits of Highly Effective People by Stephen R. Covey** - which outlines the principles and practices that lead to personal and professional success.
- **Think and Grow Rich by Napoleon Hill** - which reveals the secrets and strategies of the most successful and wealthy people in history.
- **The Alchemist by Paulo Coelho** - which tells the story of a young man who follows his dream and discovers his destiny.
- **The Four Agreements by Don Miguel Ruiz** - which explains the ancient wisdom of the Toltec culture and how to apply it to your life.

Some other ways to develop the mindset of freedom are:

imagine you're about to embark on a cosmic journey to unlock the mindset of freedom, and here are a few creative pits stops along the way:

Meditate regularly: Picture this as a daily cosmic ritual, a rendezvous with the universe where you calm your mind, focus your attention, and tap into the hidden depths of your thoughts and emotions. It's like a cosmic spa day for your mind, helping you break free from negative thinking patterns and nurture a more positive and open mindset.

Challenge yourself: Think of this as a cosmic adventure – stepping out of your comfort zone and exploring new realms that stretch your abilities and broaden your cosmic horizons. It's the grand quest to uncover new possibilities, acquire new skills, and conquer your fears. This cosmic challenge isn't just a test; it's a confidence-boosting expedition essential for your journey towards freedom.

Surround yourself with positive and supportive people: Envision this as curating your cosmic entourage. Imagine you're assembling a cosmic dream team of individuals who radiate positivity, support, and empowerment. These are the co-stars in your cosmic drama who align with your values, cheer on your victories, and offer a cosmic shoulder during your challenges. It's like a celestial gathering of kindred spirits propelling you forward on your quest for freedom.

2

THE POWER OF MINDSET

Embrace the Magic: Nurturing a Mindset for Success

Set Out on an Adventure: Revealing the Influence of Your Mentality on Life's Fabric

Prepare yourself for a cosmic journey in this chapter, where the success and happiness you experience in life are a result of the rhythm and melody of your mindset. Learn how to cultivate a growth mindset that accepts the beauty of lifelong learning and dances fearlessly with obstacles. Break free from the bonds of self-limiting ideas to realize your infinite potential. As you discover the captivating dance of visualizing success and turning it from a dream into a concrete reality, let your imagination run wild.

What is a growth mindset and why is it important?

Ever pondered the enchantment behind a growth mindset and why it's the cosmic key to a journey filled with triumphs and resilience? Allow me to paint the picture:

A growth mindset, my friend, is akin to a cosmic symphony, a belief that your abilities and talents are like cosmic clay – ever-malleable, waiting to be shaped through the alchemy of effort, feedback, and practice. Imagine it as a dance with the cosmos, where challenges waltz in as invitations to learn and grow, not looming threats or echoes of failure. Those wielding a growth mindset pirouette through the cosmic stage, unafraid of missteps, for each stumble is a hidden lesson. Feedback?

A celestial gift! They welcome constructive criticism as stardust, refining their cosmic performances.

Now, let's delve into the cosmic importance of this mindset elixir. It's not just a philosophical concept; it's the secret sauce that propels you towards goals, helps you leap over cosmic hurdles, and wraps you in solace during setbacks. Picture this – those with a growth mindset are like cosmic magnets, drawing in motivation, resilience, and the sweet taste of success.

Enter Oprah Winfrey, the cosmic virtuoso of the growth mindset symphony. She's navigated the cosmic storm, conquered daunting obstacles, all because she clung to the belief that she crafts her destiny. Oprah dances to the rhythm of her heart, unfazed by cosmic whispers. "If you want to make a difference, be different" – her cosmic mantra. Oprah stands tall as proof of the growth mindset's cosmic prowess, demonstrating that it's not just a belief system but a celestial compass steering you towards your goals, helping you navigate cosmic obstacles, and offering solace amidst the cosmic symphony of setbacks.

Let's step into the cosmic gallery of resilience, where the stories of remarkable souls paint the canvas of perseverance:

Thomas Edison, the Luminary Maestro: Picture him in the cosmic workshop of invention, proclaiming, "I have not failed. I've just found 10,000 ways that won't work." Each experiment wasn't a failure but a cosmic step towards the birth of the light bulb, a dance with discovery through trial and error.

Malala Yousafzai, the Dream Weaver: Imagine her journey, surviving a cosmic storm – a gunshot by the Taliban. Yet, she emerged as a Nobel Peace Prize winner, a cosmic advocate for girls' education. Her mantra echoes, "One child, one teacher, one book, and one pen can change the world." A cosmic symphony of resilience.

Walt Disney, the Visionary Dreamer: Picture the cosmic tapestry of his early career, woven with rejections and failures. Fired for lacking imagination and facing a bankrupt animation studio, yet he didn't surrender. Instead, setbacks fueled his motivation, leading to the creation of a cosmic empire that continues to enchant hearts.

Marie Curie, the Radiant Explorer: Visualize her navigating the cosmic realms of science, a woman facing challenges and prejudices. Yet, she stood unyielding, making groundbreaking discoveries in radioactivity. Her cosmic mantra resounds, "Nothing in life is to be feared, it is only to be understood."

Nelson Mandela, the Resilient Luminary: Imagine his cosmic journey, spending 27 years imprisoned for activism. Yet, he didn't let his spirit shatter; instead, he used it as a cosmic opportunity to learn and grow. His cosmic wisdom lingers, "The greatest glory in living lies not in never falling, but in rising every time we fall." A cosmic dance of rising against cosmic falls.

How can I develop a growth mindset?

If you're ready to waltz into the cosmic realm of a growth mindset, remember that it won't happen overnight; it'll take conscious effort and deliberate practice to change your habits and beliefs. Here is a celestial guide to assist you along the way:

Transform "Can't" into "Can't Yet": Picture this cosmic shift as the unveiling of a new dawn. By swapping "can't" with "can't yet," you're not acknowledging limitations; instead, you're gazing into the cosmos of potential and endless possibilities.

Embrace Challenges as Cosmic Choreography: In the grand cosmic ballet, challenges aren't stumbling blocks but intricate dance moves. Instead of declaring, "This is too hard," let the cosmic melody guide you to say, "This is hard, but with effort and help, I can master it."

Celebrate the Cosmic Symphony of Progress: Imagine each step toward your goals as a celestial note in a symphony. It's not just about the final crescendo; it's about dancing along the way. Celebrate not only the outcomes but also the cosmic beauty of progress and effort. Praise yourself for daring to try, regardless of the cosmic results.

Learn from Cosmic Missteps: Think of mistakes as cosmic detours rather than dead ends. Instead of lamenting, "I failed," whisper, "I learned something." Dive into the cosmic analysis, exploring what went astray and how you can navigate the cosmic constellations better next time.

Seek Cosmic Feedback: In the celestial realm, feedback is like stardust, a catalyst for growth. Instead of dreading criticism, let it be a cosmic guide. Shift from "They don't like me" to "They are trying to help me." Listen to the cosmic whispers of others, using them as a cosmic compass for personal improvement.

Draw Inspiration from Cosmic Stars: Envision the success of others not as a cosmic threat but as a radiant constellation lighting your path. Instead of feeling inferior, say, "They are an example for me." Let their cosmic strategies and achievements be guiding stars, illuminating your own cosmic goals.

"The passion for stretching yourself and sticking to it, even (or especially) when it's not going well, is the hallmark of the growth mindset, This is the mindset that allows people to thrive during some of the most challenging times in their lives."

– Carol Dweck

What are limiting beliefs and how do they affect me?

Think of limiting beliefs as shadows – those subtle but powerful thoughts that wrap around who you are, dimming the brightness of your potential and joy. They usually show up when false ideas, negative experiences, or fears play a part, creating a sort of invisible cover over what you're capable of. These thoughts might make you doubt yourself, avoid taking chances, and settle for less than you really deserve. It's like they're whispering in your ear, making you question who you are and holding you back from what you truly deserve.

- "I'm not good enough."
- "I don't have enough time/money/resources."
- "I can't do that."
- "It's too late for me."
- "People don't like me."
- "The world is a dangerous place."

Limiting beliefs can affect you in many ways. They can lower your self-esteem, reduce your motivation, increase your stress, and prevent you from achieving your goals. They can also create a self-fulfilling prophecy, where you act in ways that confirm your beliefs and make them true.

Overcoming your limiting beliefs is not easy, but it is possible. It requires a lot of self-awareness, honesty, and courage. Here are some steps to help you overcome your limiting beliefs:

Identify your limiting beliefs: The first step is to identify and acknowledge the beliefs that are holding you back. You can do this by paying attention to your thoughts, feelings, and actions and identifying when they are negative or limiting. You can also ask yourself questions like: How do I believe myself, others, and the world? Where did these beliefs come from? How will they affect me?

Challenge your limiting beliefs: The second step involves questioning and challenging the validity and accuracy of your beliefs. You can do this by searching for evidence that contradicts or disproves your beliefs, as well as alternative explanations or perspectives. You can also ask yourself questions like, "Is this belief correct?" Is this belief helpful? What if the opposite is true? How would I react differently?

Replace your limiting beliefs with empowering ones: The third step is to replace your limiting beliefs with more positive and realistic ones that promote your development and happiness. You can accomplish this by writing affirmations or statements that reflect your new beliefs and repeating them to yourself on a regular basis. You can also ask yourself questions like, "What would I like to believe instead?" How will this belief benefit me? How can I justify this belief to myself?

"Whether you think you can,
or you think you can't–you're right."

– Henry Ford

What is visualization and why is it useful?

visualization is like painting with thoughts, crafting mental images of the future you desire. It's a magical technique that not only propels you towards your goals but also becomes a beacon of confidence and performance enhancement. Let's delve into the intricacies with an illustrative example:

Visualization works by activating the same brain regions and neural pathways that are involved in the actual execution of a task. This means that by visualizing yourself succeeding, you are training your brain and body to act as if you have already achieved your goal.

Visualization can also help you reduce your anxiety and stress, by creating a positive and relaxing mental state.

Embrace the cosmic artistry of visualization, where imagination becomes the brush and your dreams the masterpiece.

Embark on a cosmic journey of visualization by selecting a specific goal or scenario that ignites your dreams. Find a tranquil sanctuary, close your eyes, and breathe in the cosmic energy. Let your mind wander into the realms of your desires, painting the scene with vibrant hues. Engage all your senses, infusing life into the cosmic canvas with vivid details. Feel the cosmic energy coursing through your emotions and thoughts.

Repeat this cosmic dance of visualization, letting the scenes unfold like chapters in a celestial story. As you immerse yourself in this cosmic reverie, sprinkle affirmations like stardust, reinforcing the cosmic energy of your visualization. In this cosmic odyssey, your imagination becomes the guiding star, steering you towards the cosmic fulfillment of your dreams.

An example of visualization is to imagine yourself giving a speech in front of a large audience. You can visualize yourself standing on the stage, looking confident and calm, speaking clearly and persuasively, and receiving applause and praise from the listeners. You can also visualize yourself overcoming any potential challenges, such as forgetting your words, feeling nervous, or facing difficult questions. By doing this, you are preparing yourself for the actual situation, and increasing your chances of success.

Visualization has many benefits, such as:

- Gain confidence
- Decrease anxiety
- Enhance performance
- Boost your motivation
- Adopt healthier behaviors
- Increase muscle strength
- Reduce pain
- Relieve stress
- Speed up healing
- Improve prospective memory
- Spark inspiration

How can I practice visualization?

Getting into visualization is like setting sail on the seas of imagination—a practice that's not tough but requires a bit of focus. Here are some simple tips to help you navigate the waters of visualization:

1. **Pick Your Dream Destination:** Choose a specific goal or situation you want to visualize. It could be anything—running a marathon, giving a speech, or traveling the world. The clearer and more realistic, the better.
2. **Find Your Zen Spot:** Locate a quiet and comfy place where you won't be disturbed. Sit or lie down, just ensuring you're relaxed and alert.

"Offline is the new peace of mind."

3. **Close Your Eyes, Breathe Deeply:** Shut your eyes, take deep breaths, and clear your mind of distractions. Focus on your breathing to set the stage.
4. **Imagine Your Scene:** Picture yourself in the scenario you want to visualize. Engage all your senses—see, hear, feel, smell, and even taste. Pay attention to your emotions and thoughts. How do you feel? What's on your mind?
5. **Repeat Your Daydream:** Keep practicing. The more you do it, the more effective it becomes. You can also use positive statements to reinforce your visualization.

In the world of visualization, let your dreams take flight and your imagination run wild. Safe travels on your journey!

"Whatever the mind can conceive and believe,
it can achieve."

– Napoleon Hill

3

MONEY MATTERS

What is financial literacy and why is it essential for achieving financial freedom?

In the intricate tapestry of personal finance, financial literacy stands as the master key, unlocking the door to a realm of financial freedom. It goes beyond knowing the basics; it's a profound understanding and skill set that empowers individuals to navigate the complex world of money.

Financial literacy is the ability to understand and manage your money effectively. It encompasses a range of skills, including budgeting, saving, investing, debt management, and understanding various financial concepts and products.

Understanding the intricacies of personal finance is like learning the notes of a song—daunting but necessary for creating a beautiful melody of financial freedom. Financial literacy isn't just a set of skills; it's the guiding light that empowers individuals to take control of their financial journey.

Beyond the Basics:

Think of financial literacy as the map that guides you through the confusing terrain of money matters. It's not just about knowing; it's about making informed choices that shape your financial story.

Crafting a Budgetary Masterpiece:

Financial literacy is the secret sauce that turns budgeting from a chore into a creative endeavor. It helps you tell a story with your budget, not just crunch numbers. It's the tool that lets you not only track expenses but also find efficient ways to allocate your money.

Savings, the Bedrock of Security:

With financial literacy, saving money becomes an art form. It's not just about putting money aside; it's about building a foundation for emergencies, reaching financial goals, and preparing for whatever the future holds.

Investing as a Symphony:

Financial literacy transforms the intimidating world of investments into a melody of understanding. It equips you with the knowledge to make investment decisions that align with your risk tolerance and financial dreams.

Conquering the Debt Dragon:

Debt, often seen as a scary monster, becomes manageable with financial literacy. It provides not just strategies but a knight's armor against unnecessary debt. Understanding different types of debt, creating repayment plans, and avoiding the debt trap become second nature.

Guardianship of Financial Well-Being:

Financial literacy becomes your guardian angel, watching over your financial health. It empowers you to make smart decisions about insurance, taxes, and other financial matters, creating a protective shield around your financial security.

In simple terms, financial literacy is the conductor leading the orchestra of financial freedom. It's the paintbrush that adds color to your financial decisions, turning them into a masterpiece of control, stability, and fulfillment.

"Financial literacy is the foundation of financial freedom."

– Robert Kiyosaki

A sustainable budget is like a trustworthy compass guiding you through the financial landscape. It's not just a plan; it's a companion that ensures your income and expenses dance in harmony, letting you live within your means while chasing the symphony of your financial goals.

Creating a sustainable budget involves:

1. **Tracking your income and expenses**: Collect all your income sources and expenses for a specific period, such as a month, to get a clear picture of your financial flow.
2. **Categorizing your expenses**: Imagine your financial canvas divided into sections – housing, food, transportation, utilities, and entertainment. Each category contributes its unique strokes to the overall masterpiece.
3. **Setting realistic goals**: Every financial composition requires a purpose. Define your objectives, whether it's saving for a down payment on a dream home, clearing lingering debts, or constructing a robust emergency fund.
4. **Prioritizing expenses**: Identify essential expenses and discretionary spending areas. Allocate your income accordingly, ensuring

that your essential expenses are covered before allocating funds to discretionary spending.

5. **Fine-tuning and Harmony:** As any seasoned composer would attest, a masterpiece is never static. Regularly review your financial opus, fine-tuning as necessary based on the ever-changing cadence of income and expenses. It's the key to maintaining a harmonious and sustainable budget over time.

"A budget is telling your money where to go, instead of wondering where it went."

– John Maxwell

Why is investing in yourself and your skills crucial for achieving financial freedom?

Pouring resources into your personal and skill development is akin to cultivating a fruitful orchard in the landscape of your future finances. Consider yourself as the diligent gardener, nurturing the seeds of your skills and talents. This investment is not just a monetary transaction; it's a commitment to your growth, a pledge to enhance your earning potential. Picture it as a key unlocking doors to uncharted opportunities, each skill you acquire acting as a unique portal to a realm of possibilities. As you invest in yourself, you're not merely accumulating knowledge; you're fortifying the walls of your financial castle, creating a stronghold of security and prosperity.

Investing in yourself involves:

Certainly! Let's delve deeper into the realms of self-investment, exploring the multifaceted facets of education, personal development, and self-improvement:

Education - The Odyssey of Knowledge:

Embark on a journey of intellectual exploration, where education becomes the compass guiding you through uncharted territories. It's not just about earning degrees; it's about delving into the vast sea of knowledge, gaining insights, and acquiring specialized skills. Picture yourself as a scholar navigating the academic waters, discovering new horizons with each course and embracing the transformative power of learning.

Personal Development - Crafting the Hero Within:

Imagine personal development as a magical elixir, refining the very essence of who you are. This elixir enhances your communication skills, turning you into a charismatic storyteller in the narrative of your life. Sharpen your problem-solving abilities, becoming the protagonist who navigates through challenges with wit and wisdom. Cultivate leadership skills that empower you to take charge, steering the plot towards success. In the grand tapestry of your self-investment adventure, personal development is the enchanting force that shapes you into the hero of your own story.

Self-Improvement - The Ever-Evolving Arsenal:

Envision self-improvement as an ever-growing arsenal, a collection of powerful tools forged in the fires of continuous learning. Your knowledge and skills are not static; they evolve with each experience, making you more adaptable to the changing landscapes of your professional and personal life. Like a vigilant blacksmith, you craft and refine your abilities, creating mighty swords of competence and resilience. In this grand saga of self-investment, you're not a passive spectator; you're the artisan, shaping the tools that will empower you in the battles and triumphs that await.

"The best investment is in yourself.
The more you know, the more you earn."

– Warren Buffett

How can we manage debt effectively and avoid falling into the debt trap?

Imagine your financial journey as an exciting adventure, with debt looming like a challenging mountain. Effective debt management acts as your guide, helping you navigate the twists and turns of this financial terrain. Picture yourself as the fearless explorer armed with financial wisdom, overcoming obstacles, and reaching new heights by tackling each debt obstacle along the way.

The journey to conquer debt is like setting sail on a grand adventure. Let's dive deeper into the art of managing debt effectively, exploring uncharted territories with strategic prowess:

Navigating the Debt Sea:

Picture your debts as vast expanses of the ocean, with each wave representing a unique financial challenge.

Envision yourself skillfully steering your financial ship through these waters, confidently overcoming each financial hurdle.

Crafting a Debt Repayment Map:

Imagine creating a meticulously detailed map, where each debt is marked as an island presenting distinctive challenges.

Strategize by prioritizing high-interest debts, envisioning a well-planned route to conquer them first for smoother financial sailing.

Sailing Against the Current of Temptation:

Visualize the allure of sirens representing impulsive spending or unnecessary credit card usage, tempting you like strong currents.

Strengthen your resolve by picturing yourself navigating away from these tempting currents, staying on course towards financial freedom.

The Wind of Professional Guidance:

Picture seeking advice from financial experts as a favorable wind guiding your sails, providing valuable insights and support.

See a distant lighthouse symbolizing professional guidance, offering a beacon of knowledge for navigating through smoother financial waters.

Celebrating Victories on Financial Shores:

Visualize reaching financial shores, celebrating victories over conquered debts with a sense of accomplishment.

Feel the satisfaction of achieving milestones, akin to a triumphant captain returning to port after a successful journey.

"The only way to get out of debt is to spend less than you earn."

– Suze Orman

What are some tips for staying financially responsible and making wise financial decisions?

Financial responsibility is a cornerstone of financial freedom. It involves making informed decisions that align with your financial goals and long-term well-being.

Ensuring financial responsibility is like tending to the garden of financial freedom. Just as a gardener nurtures plants to bloom, you cultivate a thriving financial future through informed decisions and a keen understanding of your goals.

Consider these tips as the seeds for financial responsibility:

Cultivate Awareness:

Imagine your financial landscape as a garden, and awareness as the sunlight that nurtures it. Stay mindful of your income, expenses, and financial goals, allowing this awareness to illuminate your path to a secure financial future.

Prune Unnecessary Spending:

Picture unnecessary expenses as overgrown branches that hinder the growth of your financial garden.

Regularly trim away non-essential spending, allowing your resources to flourish in areas that truly matter.

Water Your Savings:

Envision your savings as the lifeblood of your financial garden. Regularly contribute to your savings, ensuring a constant flow that nurtures the growth of your emergency fund, future investments, and long-term goals.

Fertilize with Smart Investments:

Think of smart investments as the fertilizer that enriches your financial soil. Choose investments wisely, considering their potential to yield fruitful returns and contribute to the overall health of your financial garden.

Guard Against Financial Weeds:

Visualize financial weeds as potential risks and uncertainties. Guard your financial garden by having appropriate insurance coverage, emergency funds, and a well-thought-out financial plan to protect against unexpected challenges.

Harvest Wisely:

Picture your financial goals as the fruits of your labor. Harvest the rewards of your financial responsibility wisely, enjoying the fruits of your disciplined decisions while reinvesting in the continued growth of your financial garden.

By tending to your financial garden with these tips, you nurture a landscape that not only thrives in the present but also promises a bountiful harvest for your future financial well-being.

Where every decision you make shapes the narrative of your financial story. Picture yourself at the helm, navigating towards your dreams with purpose. Trim away unnecessary expenses like unruly hedges, creating an open space for your financial goals to flourish. Envision your savings as a lush garden, each contribution nurturing its growth for resilience in challenging times. Treat investments as seeds planted in the fertile soil of your financial garden, cultivating a diverse portfolio that blossoms with strategic decisions. Weed out financial risks with a vigilant defense, safeguarding your well-tended haven. As you reach the harvest season, savor the sweetness of accomplishments and relish the rewards of disciplined decisions. This isn't just a financial guide; it's an immersive experience where you are the hero, actively shaping a prosperous and fulfilling financial future.

4

HUSTLE AND GRIT

What are side hustles and how can they contribute to financial freedom?

Side hustles, the unsung heroes of financial journeys, are the extra gigs and income-boosting endeavors we undertake alongside our primary employment. Picture them as the versatile supporting actors in the grand production of financial freedom. These side gigs don't just add dollars to our bank accounts; they bring a myriad of benefits, such as:

Income Infusion: Think of side hustles as the financial nutrients enriching your income soil. They're not just a cash boost; they're the extra green that helps pay off debts, build savings, and fund those dreams you tucked away.

Passion Ventures: Your side hustle isn't just a job; it's a canvas for your passions and skills. Imagine turning your love for photography, writing, or crafting into a profitable venture. It's not just about the extra dollars; it's about finding fulfillment in what you love.

Portfolio Building: Consider your side hustle as the bricks for your career mansion. Every project adds a layer to your professional portfolio. Whether you're a freelancer, consultant, or creative genius, these gigs enrich your skill set, making you a powerhouse in your field.

Independence Avenue: Side hustles pave the road to financial autonomy. They're not just an extra gig; they're a safety net, reducing your reliance on a single income source. Picture financial stability as a journey, and side hustles are the versatile travel companions ensuring you reach your destination resiliently and independently.

Side hustles come in a wide variety of forms, ranging from traditional part-time jobs to online freelancing, entrepreneurial ventures, and creative pursuits. The specific side hustle that suits an individual will depend on their interests, skills, and available time.

"Your side hustle is a stepping stone to your dream job."

– Mark Cuban

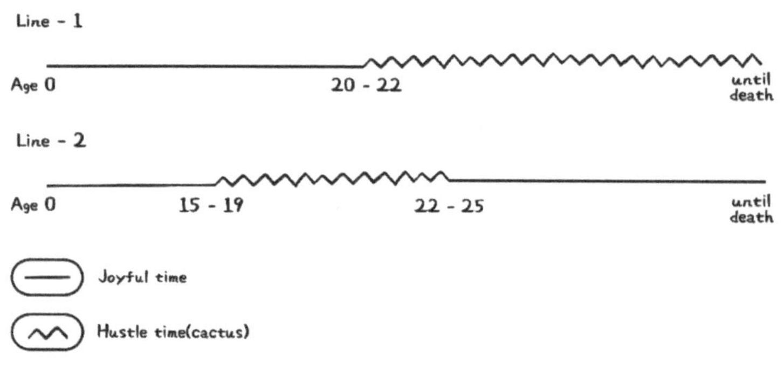

Line-2 has the advantage of having an emergency team that called **PARENTS**

You have the option to restart the game If you have line-2

But the things of disappointment are that everyone follow line two

NOW, my question is to you, What is your line?

How can we identify and pursue side hustles that align with our passions and skills?

Embarking on the journey to identify and pursue side hustles that align with your passions and skills is like crafting a personalized roadmap to your own success. Imagine yourself as an intrepid explorer of possibilities, equipped with a toolkit comprising self-reflection, research, skill development, testing, and the invaluable compass of networking.

Picture the process as a treasure hunt, with each step leading you closer to hidden gems of opportunities. Visualize these opportunities as precious artifacts that not only align with your passions but also showcase your unique set of skills.

Envision yourself in a vibrant marketplace, where potential side hustles are laid out like an array of diverse offerings. As you navigate through this bustling space, let your instincts guide you toward the stalls that resonate with the melody of your interests and the rhythm of your capabilities.

See the identification of side hustles as an art form. Imagine yourself as a skilled curator, carefully selecting pieces that complement the gallery of your skills and passions. Each hustle becomes a brushstroke on the canvas of your professional journey, contributing to a masterpiece that reflects your authentic self.

This exploration is not just a practical endeavor; it's a creative process. By infusing imagination into your search, you transform it into a captivating adventure, where the pursuit of side hustles becomes a delightful journey of self-expression, growth, and fulfillment.

Embarking on the journey to identify and pursue side hustles that align with your passions and skills is akin to peeling back the layers of your own story.

Self-reflection:

Begin in the quiet sanctuary of self-reflection, where you immerse yourself in the tapestry of your interests, hobbies, and skills. Visualize this process as a meditative exploration, unlocking the treasure trove of activities that bring you joy and the skills at which you naturally excel. Picture each revelation as a luminescent thread weaving into the fabric of your unique identity.

Research and exploration:

Venture into the vast landscape of opportunities through a journey of research and exploration. Envision yourself as a digital nomad navigating bustling marketplaces, both online and offline, filled with diverse side hustle opportunities. Imagine these platforms as vibrant bazaars, each stall offering a unique chance to align your passions and skills with meaningful ventures.

Skill development:

In the atelier of your personal and professional growth, invest in developing new skills or refining existing ones. Picture yourself as an artist, each skill acquired or enhanced a brushstroke on the canvas of your capabilities. Envision your skillset evolving into a palette, making you more adept and marketable for the specific side hustles that resonate with your journey.

Testing and experimentation:

Enter the dynamic theater of testing and experimentation, where you try on different roles and scenarios. Visualize this stage as an actor's rehearsal space, exploring various acts to discover what resonates with you and where your true strengths lie. Picture each trial as a scene in the grand play of your professional narrative.

Networking and seeking guidance:

Navigate the landscape of connections as if you're on a collective journey, surrounded by mentors and fellow travelers in the realm of side hustles. Imagine networking events and mentorship opportunities as gatherings around a bonfire, where stories are shared, advice is imparted, and insights illuminate your path. See yourself forging connections with experienced individuals, each interaction adding a chapter to your own side hustle narrative.

In this odyssey of identifying and pursuing side hustles, you aren't just a seeker; you're the author of your narrative, crafting a story of passion, skill, and success.

In this artistic fusion of passion and proficiency, your side hustle becomes more than just a pursuit; it becomes a manifestation of your authentic self, resonating with both the creator and the audience. Each endeavor is a brushstroke, each challenge an opportunity, and the entire canvas a testament to the beauty of aligning passion and skill in the pursuit of success.

> *"The best way to find your passion is to find something you're willing to work hard at."*
>
> – Oprah Winfrey

How can we embrace failure and learn from setbacks in our side hustle endeavors?

Embracing failure in the realm of side hustles is akin to navigating through stormy seas; it's not about avoiding the waves, but learning to ride them. Let's embark on a journey of resilience and growth in the face of setbacks:

Failure as a symphony of feedback:

Envision failure as a musical composition, each setback a note contributing to the melody of your entrepreneurial journey. Rather than a discordant sound, see it as feedback that orchestrates a harmonious tune of improvement. Just as a composer refines their piece, view setbacks as cues to fine-tune your approach.

Analyzing the canvas of setbacks:

Picture your side hustle as a canvas, setbacks as unexpected strokes of paint. Instead of seeing a ruined painting, analyze the colors that didn't blend well. Delve into the details of the situation, exploring the nuances that contributed to the setback. Like an artist refining their technique, use this analysis to evolve and create a more vibrant masterpiece.

Adapting with the fluidity of setbacks:

Visualize setbacks as the unpredictable currents of a river. Rather than resisting, become a skilled navigator.

Adapt and adjust your strategies, products, or services, steering your entrepreneurial boat through the turbulent waters. The ability to flow with the currents of setbacks transforms them into opportunities for navigation and growth.

Seeking the constellations of support:

Imagine setbacks as cloudy skies, hindering your view of the stars. Seek support from mentors and advisors who act as celestial navigators, guiding you through the entrepreneurial cosmos. Their wisdom and encouragement become the constellations that illuminate your path, even in the darkest of setbacks.

The dance of persistence and perseverance:

Picture persistence and perseverance as a rhythmic dance. Setbacks are just momentary pauses; your dance continues. The ability to learn from mistakes and keep dancing in the face of adversity is the choreography of success. Embrace each setback as a step in this dance, knowing that the next move brings you closer to triumph.

In this artistic interpretation of failure, setbacks become strokes, notes, and currents that contribute to the masterpiece of your side hustle journey. Each setback is not an end but a brushstroke on the canvas of your entrepreneurial narrative, adding depth, texture, and resilience to your story.

"It's not about how many times you fall.
It's about how many times you get back up."

– Winston Churchill

What are the key characteristics of a successful side hustle entrepreneur?

Successful side hustle entrepreneurs embody a symphony of characteristics, crafting a unique melody of achievement and resilience:

Passion that fuels the flame:

Imagine passion as the flame that ignites their side hustle journey. Successful entrepreneurs don't merely work; they dance with their passion, letting it illuminate the path to success. Picture them as artists painting their canvas with strokes of enthusiasm, creating a masterpiece that resonates with authenticity.

Discipline as the captain's compass:

Envision discipline as the captain's compass guiding the ship through uncharted waters. Successful side hustlers navigate with purpose and determination, steering through the waves of challenges. See them as captains of their destiny, disciplined in their actions and steadfast in their pursuit of entrepreneurial horizons. Just like a compass helps a captain stay on course, discipline helps side hustlers resist temptation and stay focused on their goals, even when the going gets tough. Remember, discipline is a muscle that can be strengthened over time, so the more you practice it, the easier it will be to achieve your side hustle dreams.

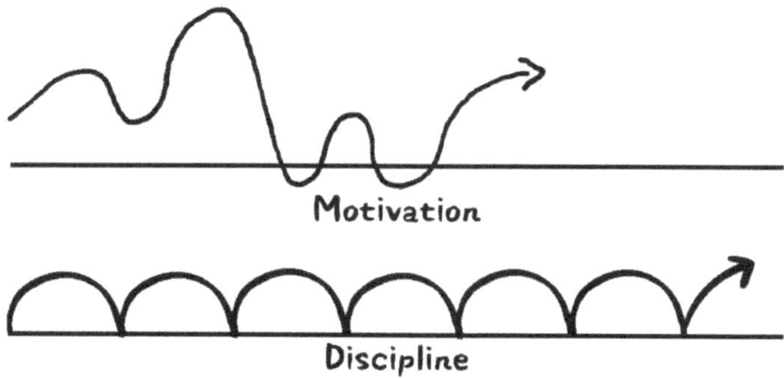

Adaptability, the shape-shifter:

Picture adaptability as a shape-shifter, enabling entrepreneurs to transform with the evolving landscape of their side hustle. Like chameleons blending into their surroundings, successful individuals seamlessly adapt to changing circumstances. See them as agile dancers, effortlessly moving through the rhythm of uncertainties.

Resilience as the armor of triumph:

Visualize resilience as an armor that shields entrepreneurs from the arrows of setbacks. Successful side hustlers wear resilience like a knight's armor, standing tall in the face of adversity. Imagine them as warriors, their armor adorned with the scars of challenges, each mark a testament to their unwavering spirit.

Lifelong learning, the fountain of wisdom:

Envision lifelong learning as a fountain, continually nourishing the minds of successful entrepreneurs. They are perpetual students, eagerly absorbing knowledge and insights. Picture them as scholars in the university of experience, their quest for wisdom propelling them towards innovation and growth.

Effective planning, the architect's blueprint:

Picture effective planning as the blueprint of a skilled architect, meticulously designing the structure of success. Successful side hustlers are architects of their destiny, crafting plans with precision. Imagine them as builders, each decision a brick in the construction of their entrepreneurial empire.

Execution, the choreography of success:

Visualize execution as a well-choreographed dance, where every move is deliberate and impactful. Successful entrepreneurs are dancers on the stage of their side hustle, turning plans into actions with grace and precision. See them as conductors, orchestrating success with each step of their entrepreneurial dance.

In this creative rendition, successful side hustle entrepreneurs are artists, captains, dancers, warriors, scholars, architects, and conductors—all weaving a tapestry of triumph with the threads of passion, discipline, adaptability, resilience, lifelong learning, effective planning, and execution.

"The only way to do great work is to love what you do."

– Steve Jobs

How can we balance our side hustles with our personal and professional lives?

Certainly! Balancing side hustles with personal and professional commitments is like creating a beautiful painting or conducting an orchestra. Here are some simple and creative tips to make it easier:

Setting Clear Boundaries:

Think of boundaries as lines on a canvas. Picture yourself as an artist creating clear lines between your side hustle, personal time, and work. Each line represents a clear boundary to keep everything in balance.

Managing Time Like a Conductor:

Imagine managing time as directing an orchestra. Picture yourself as the conductor, guiding your day's rhythm. Each task is like a note, creating a symphony where side hustles, personal moments, and work seamlessly blend.

Prioritizing Like a Sculptor:

See prioritization as a sculptor shaping your day. Visualize yourself carving out time for your side hustle, personal activities, and work. Each decision is a carve, forming a balanced sculpture reflecting your life.

Navigating with Self-Awareness:

Think of self-awareness as a compass guiding you. Picture yourself as a captain, steering through responsibilities with awareness. Each direction on the compass is a mindful choice, ensuring a journey that includes side hustles, personal joys, and work.

Finding Rest and Rejuvenation:

Imagine rest as an oasis in a busy desert. See yourself as a traveler taking a break at the oasis. Each moment of rest is like a sip of rejuvenation, giving you energy for your side hustles, personal moments, and work.

Embracing Flexibility:

Envision flexibility as a dance. Picture yourself moving gracefully between side hustles, personal activities, and work. Each step is a flexible response, helping you navigate the dance of life effortlessly.

In this simple interpretation, balancing side hustles with personal and professional life becomes a creative process—an artwork where boundaries are drawn, time is orchestrated, priorities are sculpted, self-awareness is the guide, rest is treasured, and flexibility is embraced.

Life = Work + Passion

In this uncomplicated equation, "Life" represents the delicate balance we seek. "Work" signifies our professional commitments, and "Passion" embodies the personal pursuits and side hustles that fuel our enthusiasm. The equation suggests that a well-adjusted life is achieved by harmonizing the demands of work with the fulfillment derived from our passions. It's a straightforward formula for navigating the complexities of a balanced and satisfying existence.

"Side hustles aren't just a means to an end; they're the secret code to unlocking your true trajectory in life, a tracer that illuminates the path to your full potential."

5

DIGITAL AGE OPPORTUNITIES

The digital age has opened the gates to an era brimming with possibilities, reshaping the very fabric of our lives, work, and global interactions. In this chapter, we embark on a journey delving into the boundless opportunities that the digital landscape unfolds. Here, individuals are empowered to not only embrace but also wield technology as a formidable tool for nurturing both personal and professional growth.

How can the digital age empower individuals to pursue their passions and build fulfilling careers?

In the symphony of the digital age, where information, resources, and opportunities flow freely, individuals are no longer bound by traditional barriers. This liberation allows them to embark on a journey to pursue their passions and weave fulfilling careers. As we step into this boundless realm, let's uncover some inventive strategies to artfully leverage the digital age for the fulfillment of our professional aspirations:

1. Get Social, literally:

Dive into the social media scene! It's not just for memes; connect with the cool cats in your industry, maybe even your future boss. It's like networking, but with emojis.

2. Craft Your Digital Show-and-Tell:

Think of your online portfolio as your brag board. Show off those skills, projects, and victories like trophies on a shelf. Make it so engaging that employers can't resist sliding into your DMs.

3. Be the Rockstar of Your Own Online Concert:

Ever thought of yourself as a brand? Now's the time! Rock the online world with your professional website or blog. Join virtual communities, share your wisdom, and become the rockstar you were meant to be.

4. Work in Your Pajamas (Almost):

Remote work isn't just a trend; it's a lifestyle. Picture this: you, in your comfy PJs, collaborating with talented folks from around the globe. No need to punch in at a physical office; your passport is now your workspace.

In this digital adventure, you're not just navigating a career landscape; you're embarking on a thrilling journey where every click, post, and connection propels you towards a fulfilling career. Let's make your digital footprint as irresistible as cat videos on the internet!

"The future of work is not about what you do,
but how you do it."

– Bill Gates

How can the digital age enhance financial literacy and empower individuals to make informed financial decisions?

The digital age has revolutionized access to financial information and tools, enabling individuals to make informed financial decisions and achieve their financial goals. Here are some strategies to enhance financial literacy:

Utilize financial apps and tools: Leverage budgeting apps, investment platforms, and financial planning tools to track your finances, manage your investments, and make informed decisions.

Follow reputable financial sources: Stay informed about financial trends, investment opportunities, and economic developments by following credible financial news sources, blogs, and podcasts.

Engage in online financial education courses: Enroll in online financial literacy courses to gain a comprehensive understanding of personal finance, investing, and wealth management.

Seek guidance from financial professionals: Consider consulting with a financial advisor to develop a personalized financial plan tailored to your specific needs and goals.

Enhance financial literacy for younger generations: Promote financial education among younger individuals through engaging online resources, interactive games, and age-appropriate financial literacy programs.

"Financial literacy is the key to financial freedom."

– Robert Kiyosaki

How can entrepreneurs harness the power of digital technology to launch and grow their businesses?

The In the fascinating realm of the digital age, imagine financial literacy as your superhero cape, ready to empower you to make savvy money moves. The tech revolution has turned financial wisdom into a digital feast, offering a buffet of strategies to supercharge your money game.

Embark on a digital odyssey by crafting a captivating online realm! Picture your website or e-commerce platform not as a static showcase but as a dynamic stage where your products or services take center spotlight. Envision it as a bustling marketplace, each click leading customers through an immersive journey into your brand's narrative.

Now, let's dive into the social media symphony. Instead of viewing it as a marketing tool, imagine social media platforms as vibrant canvases where your brand's story unfolds. Engage with customers not just as consumers but as co-creators, making your brand a part of their digital experience.

In the realm of digital marketing, don the hat of a strategist. See search engine optimization (SEO) not as mere techniques but as spells that elevate your brand's visibility in the vast digital forest. Picture pay-per-click (PPC) advertising as a cosmic dance of stars, each click propelling your brand into the digital galaxy. Email marketing becomes a symphony of personalized notes, resonating with your audience on a profound level.

Enter the cloud, a realm where your business tools are not just utilities but magical artifacts. Imagine customer relationship management (CRM) tools as navigational compasses, guiding your interactions with precision. Picture project management tools as wizards, orchestrating tasks seamlessly, and communication tools as conduits connecting your team across the digital landscape.

And finally, step into the e-commerce cosmos. Visualize your products not as commodities but as emissaries, reaching global customers through the digital marketplace. Every transaction isn't just a sale; it's a cosmic exchange connecting your brand with patrons worldwide. In this digital voyage, every element becomes a pixel in the masterpiece of your online brand!

"The greatest entrepreneurs are those who see opportunities where others see problems."

– Henry Ford

How can the digital age empower individuals to contribute to social impact and global change?

The In the symphony of the digital age, individuals wield instruments of connectivity, collaboration, and positive change. Imagine the digital realm not as a mere platform but as a vast, pulsating nexus where individuals become architects of societal transformation. Visualize the tools not as static implements but as dynamic extensions of one's influence, shaping the narrative of social impact.

Picture the act of connecting in the digital age as weaving threads into a tapestry of shared ideals. It's not just about networking; it's about creating a digital ecosystem where ideas converge, sparking flames of collective passion. See collaboration not as a transaction but as a communal dance, each participant contributing their unique steps to a choreography of change.

Now, envision making a positive impact as not a solitary endeavor but a collective endeavor amplified by the digital megaphone. It's not about shouting into the void; it's about resonating with a global audience, fostering a ripple effect of inspiration and change. See the digital tools as not just facilitators but catalysts, propelling individual efforts into a crescendo of global impact.

In this digital ballet, every individual becomes a dancer, pirouetting through the digital stage of social impact. It's not just about making a mark; it's about choreographing a legacy that transcends boundaries and resonates across the digital spectrum. The digital age isn't just a tool; it's a canvas, and each digital act becomes a brushstroke in the masterpiece of societal change.

In the digital age, individuals wield potent instruments to forge connections, engage in collaborative efforts, and effect positive societal change. Here are pathways through which one can actively contribute to social impact:

1. Digital Philanthropy: Illuminating Paths of Impact

In the dynamic landscape of the digital age, imagine the boundless potential to not only navigate the online realm but also to become a catalyst for positive societal change. Visualize yourself as a digital philanthropist, extending support to organizations championing social justice, environmental sustainability, or community development. Your contributions, whether in the form of donations or volunteered time and skills, ripple through the digital fabric, creating waves of impact.

2. Crafting Narratives: Your Content, Your Cause

Now, envision your expertise or passions as tools for crafting a narrative that transcends borders. As a content creator in the digital age, you have the power to produce engaging blogs, captivating videos, or compelling social media campaigns. Each creation serves as a beacon, illuminating crucial issues, fostering awareness, and igniting the spark that leads to collective action.

3. Tech for Good: Navigating Digital Solutions for Social Impact

Step into the role of a tech-savvy changemaker, exploring opportunities to harness technology for social good. Picture yourself developing or utilizing tech applications that address social challenges, promote environmental sustainability, or enhance access to education and healthcare. In this digital landscape, your technological endeavors transcend mere convenience; they evolve into meaningful contributions that leave a lasting imprint on the tapestry of societal progress.

"The best way to predict the future is to create it."

– Peter Drucker

How can the digital age facilitate lifelong learning and personal growth?

In the digital era, the adventure of learning unfolds like a captivating story, offering a treasure trove of knowledge and personal development. Dive into the realm of lifelong learning with these strategies that are akin to discovering hidden gems in the vast landscape of education.

1. E-Learning Odyssey: Charting New Horizons in the Digital Realm

Embark on a journey of perpetual discovery by leveraging the wonders of online learning platforms. Enroll in courses, tutorials, and certifications that act as portals to new skills, knowledge, and unexplored fields, weaving a lifelong tapestry of learning.

2. Digital Cohorts: Orchestrating Collective Wisdom in Online Communities

Join the symphony of digital connectivity in online communities, where engaging in forums, discussion groups, and social media connects you with kindred spirits. Here, the exchange of ideas becomes a harmonic melody, resonating with shared experiences and collective wisdom.

3. Byte-Sized Brilliance: Unveiling the Magic of Micro-Learning

In the age of micro-learning, savor the bite-sized brilliance of short-form educational formats. Delve into the world of online videos, podcasts, and infographics, where knowledge and skills unfold in compact, time-efficient parcels, fitting seamlessly into the cadence of your life.

4. Digital Passions Unleashed: Crafting Growth Through Online Pursuits

Unleash the magic of learning in the pursuit of personal interests and hobbies. Dive into the rich reservoir of online resources, communities, and interactive platforms that transform your passions into portals of personal growth and fulfillment.

5. Mindful Bytes: Navigating Inner Realms in the Digital Age

Guide your journey with mindfulness and self-reflection, seamlessly integrated into the digital realm. Explore the serenity of guided meditations, cultivate mindfulness through apps, and embrace moments of self-reflection, nurturing not just your mind but your holistic well-being in the vast landscape of lifelong learning.

"The only true education is in your own hands."

– Martin Luther King Jr.

How can the digital age promote global collaboration and cross-cultural understanding?

In the digital age, the global village is at our fingertips, fostering collaboration and cultural exchange like never before. Digital platforms break down borders, connecting individuals across continents and promoting a rich tapestry of global collaboration. Let's explore strategies that harness the power of the digital realm to enhance cross-cultural understanding:

1. Virtual Crossroads: Navigating Global Connections

Embrace virtual platforms that facilitate cross-cultural interactions, fostering meaningful connections that transcend geographical boundaries. From language exchange forums to international interest groups, the digital realm becomes a bustling crossroads for diverse perspectives.

2. Cultural Cross-Pollination: Sharing Stories in Cyberspace

Leverage digital storytelling to share cultural narratives, traditions, and experiences. Blogs, podcasts, and social media become vibrant canvases where individuals paint their cultural stories, enriching the collective narrative and promoting a deeper understanding of diverse backgrounds.

3. Language Bridges: Breaking Barriers Through Digital Dialogues

Explore language-learning apps, online language exchange programs, and multilingual forums to bridge linguistic gaps. In the digital age, language becomes a powerful tool for fostering cross-cultural communication and understanding.

4. Global Webinars: Knowledge Diplomacy in the Digital Arena

Engage in and host virtual webinars that bring together experts and enthusiasts from different corners of the globe. From discussions on cultural nuances to collaborative projects, webinars become digital amphitheaters for global learning and understanding.

5. Social Media Diplomacy: Building Bridges, Not Walls

Leverage social media as a diplomatic tool to build bridges of understanding. Engage in respectful dialogues, share diverse perspectives, and participate in global conversations that transcend cultural differences. Social media becomes a digital agora for fostering mutual respect and appreciation.

In this digital age, the world becomes not just interconnected but interwoven, creating a global tapestry where collaboration and cross-cultural understanding flourish.

"Culture is the bridge that connects people."

– Fela Kuti

How can the digital age enhance access to information and knowledge for individuals worldwide?

In the symphony of the digital age, access to information and knowledge takes center stage, empowering individuals across the globe. Let's dive into the ways the digital landscape becomes a vast library, offering an enriching experience for seekers of wisdom:

1. Digital Libraries: Where Bytes Transform into Knowledge

In the enchanted realm of the digital age, imagine a magical library where information dances to the rhythm of your curiosity. Picture yourself strolling through web pages, each click opening a door to a world of wonders. This isn't your ordinary library; it's a digital wonderland where knowledge wears the cloak of pixels and pages turn with a click.

2. Podcast Universes: Auditory Odyssey of Insights

Now, let's embark on an auditory odyssey through the podcast universes. Imagine turning mundane moments into adventures, plugging into a world where experts whisper secrets, stories unfold in your ears, and insights bloom like flowers in spring. Podcasts aren't just audio; they're portals to realms of wisdom waiting to be explored.

3. Webinars: The Digital Amphitheater of Learning

In this digital amphitheater called webinars, envision yourself sitting front row to a global dialogue. Experts from every corner of the world gather on screens, sharing their knowledge. You're not just a spectator; you're part of an interactive show, asking questions, absorbing insights, and contributing to a global symphony of learning.

4. Interactive Infographics: Visualizing Knowledge

Now, let's dive into the world of interactive infographics. Imagine turning complex ideas into vibrant visual art. Here, information isn't confined to paragraphs; it transforms into colorful illustrations, making learning an adventure for the eyes. Complex concepts become visual stories, engaging and captivating your imagination.

5. Virtual Mentorship: Wisdom Shared Across Screens

In the virtual mentorship realm, envision a space where wisdom seekers connect with mentors across screens. It's not just advice; it's a digital mentorship dance. Here, knowledge isn't a guarded secret; it's a gift shared generously, creating a culture where mentorship knows no borders.

In the digital age, information isn't a dry collection of facts; it's a vibrant tapestry of stories waiting to be unfolded. Each click, each listen, and each interaction is a chapter in your digital adventure, where knowledge isn't just accessible; it's a magical story waiting to be explored.

"Information is the most powerful asset of the 21st century."

– Bill Gates

How can the digital age foster innovation and entrepreneurship in developing countries?

1. Unveiling the Digital Canvas: Igniting Innovation in Developing Lands

In the digital age, imagine a vast canvas stretching across developing countries, waiting to be painted with strokes of innovation. It's not just a canvas; it's a playground where the spirit of entrepreneurship dances with the winds of change.

2. Digital Seeds of Innovation: Cultivating Creativity in Developing Soils

Picture digital seeds scattered across landscapes, sprouting into innovative blooms. These aren't ordinary seeds; they carry the essence of ideas, nurtured by the fertile soil of connectivity. In the digital age, innovation isn't a distant dream; it's a garden flourishing in the hearts of entrepreneurs.

3. The Entrepreneurial Symphony: Orchestrating Opportunities in Digital Harmonies

Now, imagine a symphony echoing through digital corridors. Entrepreneurs in developing countries aren't soloists; they're part of a grand orchestra, each note resonating with the opportunities presented by the digital age. It's not just about entrepreneurship; it's about creating a harmonious melody of progress.

4. Digital Marketplaces: Bazaars of Innovation and Opportunity

Step into the bustling bazaars of digital marketplaces in developing lands. Here, innovation isn't confined to workshops; it's showcased on virtual stalls, attracting global attention. It's not just a marketplace; it's a vibrant carnival where ideas twirl and dance, capturing the imagination of the world.

5. Digital Bridges to Global Shores: Navigating Entrepreneurial Journeys

Envision digital bridges spanning across oceans, connecting entrepreneurs in developing countries to global shores. It's not just a bridge; it's a navigational route for entrepreneurial journeys, where ideas sail freely, reaching distant lands and creating waves of innovation.

In the digital age, innovation and entrepreneurship in developing countries aren't just possibilities; they're stories unfolding, adventures waiting to be written on the digital canvas of progress.

"Innovation is the ability to see change
as an opportunity - not a threat."

– Steve Jobs

Sometimes

Growth means

Leaving people behind

6

NETWORKING AND MENTORSHIP

Why is networking important for young people seeking financial independence?

In the world of connections, networking is like a dance, allowing you to build relationships with those who share your dreams. For those striving for financial independence, it's a treasure chest full of benefits.

In the intricate world of connections, networking becomes a dance, expanding your circle and introducing you to a diverse cast of characters. This dynamic process offers a treasure trove of benefits for those aspiring to financial independence:

1. Expanding Your Circle: Unveiling New Horizons

Networking is your backstage pass to a diverse symphony of backgrounds and expertise. It's the art of connecting with individuals whose stories broaden your perspective, unveiling new horizons and opportunities.

2. Gaining Insights and Knowledge: Mentors as Maestros

Amidst the networking dance, mentors and peers take center stage, offering insights into various industries, financial markets, and entrepreneurial realms. Their experiences and wisdom act as the guiding notes that help you compose informed decisions and sidestep common pitfalls.

3. Discovering Untapped Opportunities: The Serendipity Waltz

Networking isn't just a dance; it's a serendipitous journey. It can unveil hidden job openings, investment prospects, or collaborations that dwell in the shadows, waiting to be discovered by those attuned to the rhythm of opportunity.

4. Building Credibility and Trust: The Trust Tango

As you weave through the intricate steps of networking, a foundation of credibility and trust emerges. Your network becomes a testament to your character, making it easier to secure funding, partnerships, or clients as you perform the trust tango.

5. Finding Like-Minded Individuals: The Community Waltz

In the grand ballroom of networking, you discover partners in the dance who share your passion for financial independence and entrepreneurial dreams. This connection forms a community, a support system that resonates with motivation, encouragement, and shared aspirations.

Networking isn't merely about gathering business cards or navigating industry events—it's about fostering genuine connections and mutually enriching relationships. Picture it as a vibrant garden where each connection is a unique blossom contributing to the beauty and vitality of the whole. By weaving an intricate tapestry of engagement, you cultivate a network not just for the sake of it, but as a living, breathing entity ready to support and uplift you on your journey towards financial independence.

"Networking is not about collecting business cards, it's about connecting with people."

– Michael Hyatt

How can young people identify and connect with potential mentors?

Finding Embarking on the journey to financial independence is like setting sail in uncharted waters, and having mentors on board is like navigating with seasoned captains. Let's explore some creative ways to uncover and forge connections with these mentors who can be your guiding stars:

1. **Trailblazing Events:** Picture yourself at industry gatherings or professional soirees, where seasoned individuals stand as beacons of wisdom. Attend these events with the eagerness of a seeker, collecting gems of insight from those who've treaded the financial waters before you.

2. **Digital Discovery:** Imagine online platforms like LinkedIn as a treasure map leading you to potential mentors. Dive into this digital sea, reaching out to individuals whose experiences resonate with your aspirations. Craft personalized messages, turning this digital journey into meaningful connections.

3. **Workshops and Seminars:** Envision workshops and seminars as enchanted forests, where you might chance upon wise mentors sharing their secrets. Attend these events with an open mind, ready to absorb the

wisdom that could illuminate your path to financial independence.

4. Proactive Networking: In the realm of mentorship, waiting is not an option. Picture yourself as an initiator, reaching out to individuals you admire. Approach this proactive networking with genuine curiosity, expressing your eagerness to learn from their experiences.

5. Enthusiastic Engagement: When connecting with potential mentors, think of it as a shared adventure. Prepare to articulate your goals, dreams, and what you hope to gain from their mentorship. Let your enthusiasm be the spark that ignites meaningful connections on this exciting journey.

Discovering the perfect mentor is akin to unlocking a game-changing level. Actively seeking seasoned individuals and showcasing your eagerness to learn not only forges impactful mentorship connections but also serves as a catalyst for your personal and professional growth.

"A mentor is someone who sees more
in you than you see in yourself."

– Bob Proctor

What are some key qualities to look for in a mentor?

When embarking on the quest for a mentor to guide you on the path to financial independence, consider these qualities that can shape a transformative mentorship experience:

1. Experience and Expertise:

Delve into the realm of mentors with a rich tapestry of success in the field you're venturing into. Choosing a mentor with a well-established track record ensures you benefit from their seasoned experience, gaining insights that can steer you away from common pitfalls.

2. Willingness to Share Knowledge:

Seek a mentor whose generosity in sharing knowledge knows no bounds. A mentor should not only possess a wealth of insights but also have a genuine eagerness to contribute to your growth and success. Their willingness to share experiences becomes a guiding light on your journey.

3. Effective Communication Skills:

Envision a mentor who paints a clear picture through effective communication. Whether it's delivering concise explanations, offering constructive feedback, or providing uplifting encouragement, a mentor with strong communication skills becomes a beacon in your mentorship voyage.

4. Strong Interpersonal Skills:

Imagine a mentor who not only imparts wisdom but also excels in building connections. Strong interpersonal skills allow a mentor to weave a fabric of trust, creating a conducive environment for open dialogue and meaningful learning experiences.

5. Alignment with Your Values:

Ensure your mentorship compass aligns with your core values. A mentor whose values resonate with your own becomes more than a guide; they become a companion on your journey. Shared beliefs create a foundation for a robust and harmonious mentorship relationship.

Selecting the perfect mentor is akin to choosing a guiding star for your financial journey. Imagine this mentor not merely as a source of guidance but as an inspiration, illuminating your path to financial independence. As you navigate uncharted territories, envision your mentor as a compass, enriching your journey with invaluable experiences. Wisely chosen, your mentor becomes the beacon lighting the way to your financial goals.

"A mentor is someone who allows you to see places in yourself you never knew existed."

– Oprah Winfrey

How can young people make the most of their mentorship relationships?

Picture it as a dance of guidance, where the steps you take can shape the rhythm of success. Ready to turn this mentorship journey into an adventure? Here's your guide:

1. Define Your Dreams Loud and Clear:

Imagine sharing your dreams and aspirations like opening a treasure map. The clearer you are with your mentor, the more customized their guidance can be. It's like handing them the key to your unique kingdom.

2. Ask Questions That Spark a Symphony:

Ever thought of your questions as the notes that compose a beautiful melody? Craft them thoughtfully, let them resonate during conversations, and watch as your mentorship duet turns into a harmonious exchange of wisdom.

3. Create a Learning Playground:

Imagine a classroom where both sides of the desk hold lessons. Mentorship is a shared learning adventure. Make room for your mentor's insights while sharing your own. Let it be a playground of ideas, a dance of perspectives.

4. Turn Mentorship Nuggets into Gold:

Think of your mentor's advice as golden nuggets on your path. The real magic happens when you turn those nuggets into actions. It's like transforming mentorship wisdom into the currency of your success.

5. Sprinkle Appreciation Pixie Dust:

Every mentorship journey deserves a touch of magic dust – gratitude. Sprinkle it generously. A simple 'thank you' can make the mentorship potion more potent, creating a positive spell for both sides.

In this mentorship fairytale, your active steps and vibrant energy can turn the pages of learning and growth. Ready to dance the mentorship waltz? The stage is yours!

"Turn every mentorship nugget into gold, and you'll find the treasure of your own success."

7

ESCAPING THE RAT RACE: CHARTING YOUR PATH TO FINANCIAL FREEDOM

Marks a pivotal chapter in our journey towards economic liberation. In this segment, we delve into strategies and insights that guide you away from the monotonous routine and towards a life where financial constraints no longer dictate your choices.

Picture this chapter as a roadmap, carefully designed to navigate the twists and turns on your way to financial freedom. We'll explore the principles of budgeting, investing, and cultivating a mindset that breaks free from the conventional expectations of the rat race.

Just as an architect drafts blueprints, here we sketch the contours of a life where your finances work for you, not the other way around. It's a journey filled with transformative decisions, strategic investments, and the gradual accumulation of wealth that empowers you to live life on your terms.

So, buckle up for a chapter that's not just about financial management but a liberation manifesto, guiding you towards a future where the rat race is merely a distant memory, and financial freedom is the reality you sculpt.

What is the rat race, and how does it limit financial freedom?

Imagine the rat race as a relentless treadmill, where you're running full tilt but going nowhere in terms of true financial freedom. It's like a never-ending loop, and breaking free from it is not just about escaping constraints but also embracing a journey towards financial liberation. Let's unravel the story of the rat race and its impact on our freedom:

1. Time Tango: Ever feel like you're dancing to the rhythm of someone else's drum in the rat race? It's a trade-off, where you exchange the beats of your passions for the monotonous ticking of the clock.

2. Income Island: The rat race often leaves us stranded on the island of a single income source. Picture it like being marooned, with waves of economic uncertainty threatening to wash away the stability of your financial shores.

3. Risk Riddles: Fear not, for in the rat race, risk is a four-letter word. It discourages us from taking the daring steps toward entrepreneurship or investing in our dreams. It's like trying to run a marathon with your shoelaces tied together.

But fear not! The tale doesn't end here. We're about to embark on an adventure that transcends the rat race, navigating uncharted waters toward financial liberation. Buckle up for a journey that's not just informative but also a thrilling escape from the mundane.

"The only way to do great work is to love what you do. If you haven't found it yet, keep looking. Don't settle."

– Steve Jobs

How can one redefine financial independence beyond material gains?

Picture financial independence not as a dull lecture but as a thrilling adventure, where the path to freedom is paved with excitement and discovery. Buckle up for a journey beyond the mundane, as we redefine financial independence in a tone that sparks curiosity and adds a dash of zest to the narrative.

1. Experiences Over Possessions Magic Show:

Get ready for a magical spectacle where experiences take the spotlight. Watch as possessions disappear, making way for a show that dazzles with the richness of life's adventures. It's not just financial wisdom; it's a captivating magic trick that enchants your perspective.

2. Below Your Means Sleight of Hand:

Imagine a masterful sleight of hand trick, where living below your means becomes a skillful act. The magician gracefully maneuvers through the intricacies of conscious financial decisions, leaving you in awe of the artistry behind the choices.

3. Streams of Income Circus Act:

Step into the grand circus tent of financial independence, where multiple streams of income perform a daring balancing act. Witness the thrill as the high wire of financial resilience is crossed, creating a spectacle that leaves you cheering for the versatility of income streams.

4. Investment Ballet of Growth:

Join the ballet of investment where every move is a step towards personal and professional growth. It's not just a dance; it's a performance that crescendos with the promise of a flourishing future. Watch as your investments pirouette towards financial empowerment.

5. Minimalist Tango of Simplicity:

Envision a tango where the minimalist leads with elegance. It's a dance that values simplicity over the extravagant twirls of excess. Feel the rhythm of a clutter-free existence, where each step is a testament to the beauty found in life's uncomplicated moments.

This isn't your average financial guidance; it's an enthralling show where each concept is a star performer, leaving you with a sense of wonder and a desire to explore the world of financial independence with a newfound excitement.

What are some alternative paths to financial freedom besides the traditional 9-to-5 career?

Embarking on the quest for financial freedom is not confined to the conventional 9-to-5 career. Let's unravel a vibrant spectrum of alternative paths, each one pulsating with unique energy and possibilities.

1. Freelance Symphony of Independence:

Picture yourself as the conductor of your work life, orchestrating a freelance symphony that harmonizes with your skills and passions. No rigid schedules, just the liberating notes of independence playing in the background.

2. Entrepreneurial Ballet of Risk and Reward:

Dive into the daring ballet of entrepreneurship, where every move carries the thrill of risk and the promise of reward. It's not a routine; it's a dance of innovation and resilience, with each pirouette taking you closer to financial autonomy.

3. Investment Jazz Ensemble:

Join the jazz ensemble of investments, where your money becomes a versatile instrument in a melody of financial growth. Watch as your portfolio plays a tune of wealth creation, improvising with the ever-changing rhythms of the market.

4. Digital Nomad Adventure:

Imagine a nomadic adventure where your office is wherever you choose it to be. The digital nomad lifestyle is a journey of remote work, global exploration, and a passport stamped with experiences. It's not just a career; it's a lifestyle of freedom.

5. Passive Income Ballet:

Step into the graceful ballet of passive income, where your money dances effortlessly even while you rest. It's a performance where investments, royalties, and streams of income twirl in unison, creating a financial ballet that requires minimal effort from you.

6. Creative Artistry in Side Hustle Theater:

Unleash your creative artistry in the side hustle theater, where your passions take center stage. It's not just a side gig; it's a performance of turning hobbies into revenue streams, transforming your interests into avenues for financial liberation.

This isn't your run-of-the-mill financial advice; it's a gallery of alternative paths painted with vibrant strokes, inviting you to explore avenues beyond the ordinary and chart your course to financial freedom with a spirit of adventure.

"The journey of a thousand miles begins with a single step."

– Lao Tzu

How can one adopt a growth mindset to embrace continuous learning and adaptability?

Imagine diving into the mindset of growth as if it were a thrilling novel, with each chapter filled with twists, turns, and character development. It's not a lecture; it's an exploration, an adventure where you're the protagonist.

1. Symphony of Self-Belief:

Picture yourself as the conductor of a symphony, where each note represents your belief in growth. You're not just learning; you're composing the soundtrack of your success story.

2. Setbacks as Plot Twists:

Life's journey is an adventure novel with unexpected plot twists. Embrace setbacks as intriguing turns that add spice to your narrative, propelling you forward in the story of your life.

3. Quest for Knowledge Treasures:

Envision a quest for knowledge treasures, like a thrilling exploration where each piece of wisdom is a valuable find. You're not just learning; you're on a treasure hunt for insights that enrich your character.

4. Dance of Adaptability:

See the dance of adaptability as a rhythmic ballet. Be open to change, letting the music guide your graceful movements. Every step is a fluid adaptation to the evolving circumstances around you.

5. Camaraderie with Growth Supporters:

Picture yourself surrounded by a supportive ensemble, a fellowship of positive individuals who applaud your every act of learning. It's not just a social circle; it's a cheer squad for your journey of growth.

In this theater of personal development, adopting a growth mindset is not a lecture; it's an enthralling play where you are the star, the scriptwriter, and the director. It's an odyssey of belief, resilience, and continuous learning, where every chapter unfolds with the excitement of a captivating narrative.

What are some practical steps one can take to start their journey towards financial freedom?

Embarking on the road to financial freedom is like stepping into a thrilling adventure, where each step is a plot twist in your own epic story. Let's ditch the textbook vibes and dive into a narrative that feels more like a page-turning novel:

1. Destination: The Quest for Clear Financial Goals

Picture yourself standing at the edge of possibility, not with a checklist, but a treasure map of dreams waiting to be uncovered.

2. Treasure Map: Budgeting, Your Personal Cartography

Think of your budget not as cold numbers but as a magical map guiding you through the twists and turns of your financial journey.

3. Frugality: Unleashing the Art of Financial Alchemy

Imagine frugality as a spell that transforms spending habits into golden opportunities, not just saving money but conjuring financial abundance.

4. Investment: Planting Seeds of Wealth

Envision your investments as seeds sown in the fertile soil of your future, not just numbers but a garden that grows with time.

5. Side Hustles: Passion Projects Shaping Your Story

See your side hustles as dynamic chapters, each adding its own flavor to the narrative, turning passions into thrilling plot twists.

6. Guides on the Journey: Financial Mentors

Imagine financial advisors as wise mentors, sharing nuggets of wisdom, not just advice but a transformational guidance for your hero's journey.

7. Economic Trends: Navigating the Financial Climate

Think of staying informed about economic trends as checking the weather forecast for your adventure, not just data but reading the signs of your financial journey.

8. Skills Development: Arming Yourself for the Adventure

Envision acquiring new skills as adding tools to your adventurer's kit, not just education but preparing for the challenges that lie ahead.

9. Mindset: The Wind in Your Financial Sails

Picture a positive mindset as the wind propelling your financial ship forward, not just a state of mind but the force that keeps you sailing through storms.

This is not a financial plan; it's an enthralling story waiting to be written. Your journey to financial freedom is not just about numbers; it's a narrative with you as the daring protagonist. So, grab your pen and let's turn the page to the next exciting chapter!

8

HEALTH IS WEALTH: FUELING YOUR JOURNEY TO FINANCIAL INDEPENDENCE

In this chapter, we're not just exploring the intersections of health and wealth; we're crafting a narrative where well-being is the backbone of financial independence. Your journey to financial freedom is not a solitary expedition; it's a collective adventure where health and wealth dance together in a flourishing partnership. So, let's embark on this chapter with the vigor of a well-nurtured spirit and the resilience of a financially empowered mind.

In the pursuit of financial independence and breaking free from the rat race, many individuals overlook the crucial aspect of health and well-being. Physical and mental health are not just prerequisites for success; they are the foundation upon which your journey towards financial freedom is built.

Why is prioritizing health essential for achieving financial independence?

In the thrilling pursuit of financial independence and escaping the relentless rat race, many forget the unsung hero – health and well-being. Think of them not as mere prerequisites for success but as the bedrock upon which your grand adventure to financial freedom unfolds.

Why is giving health the spotlight crucial for reaching financial independence? Let's explore:

1. Cost-Conscious Vitality:

Imagine a world where good health is a financial wizard, significantly reducing your healthcare costs. It's not just well-being; it's a budget-friendly magic trick, unlocking more resources for your financial conquests.

2. Productivity Power-Up:

Picture a healthy body and a sharp mind as your productivity superheroes. They swoop in, boosting efficiency and focus, allowing you to tackle financial goals with superhero-like prowess.

3. Energize Your Ambitions:

See good health as the fuel for your dreams. It's not just about physical well-being; it's a reservoir of energy and motivation that propels you toward financial success with unwavering determination.

4. Resilience Reinforcement:

Envision a healthy lifestyle as your superhero cape, enhancing your ability to bounce back from setbacks. In the financial journey, where obstacles are part of the landscape, resilience becomes your secret weapon.

5. Mindset Magic:

Consider good health the alchemist of a positive mindset and mental clarity. It's not just about feeling good; it's a mental elixir that helps you make savvy financial decisions and keeps your eyes fixed on long-term goals.

In this tale of financial liberation, health isn't a sideline character; it's the co-protagonist. As you navigate the twists and turns of financial independence, let good health be your trusted sidekick, adding flavor, vibrancy, and a touch of magic to your epic saga. It's not just about counting dollars; it's about dancing through the journey with the rhythm of well-being. So, strap in for a narrative where health and financial freedom waltz together, creating a symphony of a truly prosperous life.

Investing in your health is not just about avoiding illness; it's about empowering yourself to achieve your financial aspirations. By prioritizing your well-being, you lay the groundwork for a successful and fulfilling journey towards financial independence.

What are some practical steps to maintain physical and mental health on a tight budget?

Keeping your physical and mental well-being in top-notch condition doesn't have to be a drain on your wallet. You don't need to splurge on extravagant gym memberships or fancy supplements. Instead, embrace the simplicity of practical steps to nurture your health, even when operating on a tight budget. These are not just cost-effective measures; they're your passport to a healthy and fulfilling lifestyle without breaking the bank. Get ready for a journey where well-being meets frugality, proving that health is truly wealth on any budget.

1. Unleash Your Inner Explorer:

Dive into the rhythm of life with 30 minutes of playful, heart-thumping activities. Whether it's the brisk beat of a morning run, the serene strokes of swimming, or the freedom found on two wheels, let your body be the canvas of your movement masterpiece.

2. Feast on the Colors of Nature:

Transform your diet into a vibrant palette of colors. Savor the sweetness of fruits, embrace the crunch of vegetables, dance with whole grains, and let lean proteins take center stage. Bid farewell to the uninvited guests: unhealthy fats and processed foods.

3. Surrender to the Night's Embrace:

Let the night unfold its magic by surrendering to 7-8 hours of restful sleep. Establish a bedtime routine that's your personal lullaby, weaving dreams of rejuvenation and waking up refreshed to conquer the day.

4. Dance with the Stress Busters:

Turn stress into a waltz with daily rituals that enchant your senses. Immerse yourself in the calming symphony of yoga, find solace in the stillness of meditation, or let nature be your therapist. Stress, meet your match.

5. Tribe Vibes for Emotional Symphony:

Surround yourself with a symphony of positive vibes. Your friends and family aren't just a network; they are your orchestra of support, your cheering section, and the harmony that makes life's melody all the more beautiful.

Cultivating a healthy lifestyle shouldn't feel like a financial tightrope. Embrace the art of simple habits and tap into a treasure trove of free or budget-friendly resources. Your journey to physical and mental well-being can be both enriching and pocket-friendly.

"An investment in health is the best
investment you can make."

– Warren Buffett

How can maintaining a healthy work-life balance contribute to achieving financial independence?

A robust work-life balance isn't just a luxury; it's your golden ticket to financial independence. Here's how it becomes your secret weapon:

1. **Evading Burnout, Amplifying Productivity:** Imagine a world where burnout is banished, replaced by peak productivity. Steering clear of overwork isn't just about preventing burnout; it's a strategic move towards heightened productivity, accelerating your journey to financial goals.

2. **Pursuing Passions, Fuelling Motivation:** It's not merely about hobbies; it's a clandestine boost for your financial expedition. Envision each passion-filled moment as an investment in motivation. Allocating time to what you love isn't just about well-being; it's cashing in on a motivation windfall propelling you towards financial triumph.

3. **Nurturing Relationships, Cementing Success:** Relationships aren't just a social courtesy; they're your backstage pass to financial victory. Robust connections go beyond mere support; they form your entourage, enthusiastically cheering you on. Picture each relationship as a foundational pillar for success, a network that elevates and propels you towards financial triumph.

4. **Maintaining Positivity, Triumphing over Challenges:** Balanced living isn't just about zen moments; it's your shield for financial skirmishes. It's a positivity

elixir that clears the path, fortifies emotional resilience, and readies you to overcome financial hurdles. It's not just a lifestyle; it's your covert strategy for navigating the complexities of your financial expedition.

financial independence isn't a mere pursuit of wealth; it's a vibrant tapestry woven with balance and fulfillment. Picture this: a journey where financial triumph harmonizes with a life rich in meaning. Elevating work-life balance isn't just a strategy; it's the secret sauce that propels you towards your financial goals, ensuring that every step is laden with well-being, joy, and an unwavering zest for the journey.

How can mindfulness and meditation practices enhance your financial decision-making?

Imagine sailing through the seas of financial decisions with the wind of tranquility at your back. In this story, stress becomes a distant memory, chased away by the soothing tunes of mindfulness. It's not just about decisions; it's about crafting a financial journey guided by clear thoughts and relaxation. As the plot thickens, meditation takes center stage, revealing the hidden layers of self-awareness. It's a lantern, shining light on your values, motivations, and financial goals, transforming decision-making into a reflective adventure. Now, let's shift our focus – mindfulness practices become the trusty sidekick, honing your ability to stay in the present. No more scattered thoughts; just a spotlight on the intricate dance of financial decisions. And as the curtain falls on this mindful drama, picture making choices not just with clarity but with the calm composure of a seasoned navigator. Meditation becomes the script, helping you approach financial decisions with a sense of serene objectivity.

1. Reducing stress and anxiety:

In this serene landscape, stress gracefully bows out, leaving your financial decisions untainted by its shadows. Mindfulness techniques act as a soothing melody, promoting relaxation and fostering clear thinking.

2. Improving self-awareness:

As the journey deepens, meditation becomes a lantern, illuminating the caverns of self-awareness. It unveils your values, motivations, and financial goals, turning decision-making into an introspective voyage.

3. Enhancing focus and concentration:

Picture mindfulness practices as your trusty sidekick, training you to be present and focused. No more wandering thoughts; just a laser-sharp focus on the intricate landscape of financial decisions.

4. Promoting a sense of calm and clarity:

As the curtain falls on this mindful spectacle, envision making financial decisions not just with clarity but with the calm objectivity of a seasoned navigator. Meditation helps you approach financial decisions with a sense of calm, clarity, and objectivity.

Picture weaving the threads of mindfulness and meditation into the fabric of your daily routine, transforming financial decision-making into an art. It's not just about numbers; it's about orchestrating a symphony where each note resonates with your long-term goals and well-being. As you embrace mindfulness, imagine it as a magic wand that dispels the fog of uncertainty, allowing you to make decisions with a clarity that feels almost like a gentle breeze. Now, meditation steps onto the stage, a wise sage guiding you to a profound understanding of your financial landscape. Together, they become your trusted companions, helping you navigate the intricate dance of decisions with a harmonious blend of insight and serenity.

"The quieter you become, the more you hear."

– Ram Dass

How can prioritizing sleep contribute to your financial success?

Imagine sleep as the secret ingredient in the recipe of financial triumph, working its magic in the realms of your mind. As you venture into the land of dreams, your cognitive function is rejuvenated, like a well-tuned instrument ready to tackle the symphony of financial decisions. Picture the elusive risks and impulsive urges, mere shadows in the night when you've embraced rest, allowing your financial goals to thrive in the light of prudence. And in the quiet hours of slumber, creativity blooms like a midnight garden, offering innovative ideas that become the currency of financial independence. As you wake, basking in the morning glow, your mood is a beacon of positivity, stress dissipating like morning mist, propelling you towards success in every facet of life.

Unlocking the power of prioritizing sleep reveals a host of benefits for your financial success:

1. Enhancing Cognitive Function:

Picture sleep as the conductor of your mental orchestra, orchestrating improved memory, heightened focus, and sharper problem-solving skills. These are the essential notes in composing sound financial decisions.

2. Reducing Impulsiveness and Risk-Taking:

In the realm of sleep, impulsiveness and unnecessary risks fade into the night, ensuring your journey towards financial goals is guided by deliberate and considered choices.

3. Boosting Creativity and Innovation:

As your mind rests, creativity blossoms like a midnight garden. Well-rested, your thoughts become the seeds of innovative solutions, a valuable currency on the path to financial independence.

4. Improving Overall Mood and Well-Being:

Sufficient sleep transforms your waking hours into a canvas of positivity. Stress dissipates like morning mist, contributing to an overall sense of well-being that propels you towards success in every facet of life.

Choosing to embrace sleep as a priority is akin to investing in your own treasure trove of mental clarity, cognitive prowess, and holistic well-being—a trifecta that forms the very bedrock of your journey towards financial independence.

> *"Sleep is the golden chain that ties health and our bodies together."*
>
> – Thomas Dekker

How can creating a supportive network of friends and family contribute to your financial success?

Navigating the path to financial independence is a thrilling adventure, and building a tribe of supporters is your secret weapon for success. Imagine crafting a fellowship that goes beyond mere cheering – it's like assembling your personal Avengers team dedicated to your financial triumphs.

Now, let's delve into the dynamics of this financial Avengers team:

1. **Inspiration Unleashed:** Envision having an entourage that not only boosts your spirits but unleashes a torrent of motivation, anchoring you firmly to your financial aspirations.

2. **The Brain Trust:** Picture your inner circle not just offering emotional support but also serving as a treasure trove of financial insights – think of them as your very own financial Jedi Council, guiding you through every fiscal challenge.

3. **Emotional Resilience HQ:** Visualize a fortress where emotional support is the secret sauce, providing you with the strength to rebound from setbacks and emerge as a financial superhero, ready to face whatever financial foes come your way.

4. The Party Planners: Consider your achievements transforming into epic celebrations, with your wins becoming communal victories. These celebrations fuel your determination to conquer new financial frontiers, making every step of the journey a joyous and triumphant experience.

Building your dream team isn't just about having cheerleaders; it's like assembling your personal squad of dream architects. Imagine this: your inner circle isn't just nodding along; they're the architects sketching blueprints of your success, crafting a masterpiece of encouragement, advice, and emotional fortitude. It's not just about having supporters; it's about having dream-weavers who sprinkle motivation, turning your path to financial independence into a captivating journey. So, surround yourself with these dream alchemists and watch as they turn your aspirations into tangible, awe-inspiring realities!

"Our friends are the thermometers that tell us the temperature of our own lives."

– Mary C. Crowley

How can actively seeking guidance from financial professionals enhance your financial independence journey?

Why should you make financial professionals your go-to guides on the journey to financial independence? Well, think of it as having financial wizards on speed dial. These money maestros aren't just handing out advice; they're crafting a personalized strategy, unlocking financial superpowers you never knew existed. Forget the dull charts and graphs; this turns your financial path into a thrilling adventure. With these financial superheroes by your side, money matters become not just understandable but downright exciting.

Now, let's dig into why teaming up with financial professionals is a game-changer:

1. **Tailored Strategies:** No cookie-cutter solutions here. Financial professionals create strategies that are as unique as your financial goals, making your journey toward financial freedom feel like a custom-made suit.

2. **Navigating the Maze:** The financial world can be like a labyrinth. Financial experts act as your GPS, guiding you through the twists and turns, helping you dodge pitfalls, and making sure you stay on the right path.

3. **Spotting Opportunities:** Financial professionals have a knack for spotting opportunities that might be invisible to the naked eye. Their expertise helps you grab those chances, optimizing your financial moves for long-term success.

4. **Risk Busters:** Managing risks is a big deal in finance. Financial professionals assess and neutralize risks, making sure your financial strategies are like a superhero suit—strong, resilient, and ready for anything.

5. **Always Learning:** The financial world doesn't sit still. It's always changing. Financial professionals keep you in the loop, so you're not just keeping up; you're ahead of the curve.

6. Total Financial Game Plan: It's not just about investments. Financial professionals take a 360-degree view, considering everything from taxes to retirement. It's like having a financial GPS that covers all the routes.

In a nutshell, teaming up with financial professionals isn't just a smart move; it's like having a backstage pass to the thrilling show of your financial independence.

9

LEGACY AND IMPACT

Why is leaving a positive legacy important when pursuing financial independence?

Creating a lasting impact becomes a pivotal aspect in the pursuit of financial independence, providing you with the opportunity to:

1. **Impact Maestro:** Imagine your financial resources as the notes in a symphony, orchestrating a melody of positive change that resonates far beyond your own existence.

2. **Trailblazer's Torch:** Your journey to financial independence isn't just a path; it's a blazing trail, lighting the way for others to embark on their quests, fueled by the hope and courage you've ignited.

3. **Architect of Tomorrow:** Envision your support for causes as the architectural blueprint for a tomorrow draped in the hues of education, eco-friendliness, and social equity—a legacy building bridges to a better world.

4. **Fulfillment Alchemist:** Beyond the wealth amassed, your legacy is an alchemical elixir, infusing deeper meaning into the fabric of existence, leaving an indelible mark that stretches beyond the confines of time.

Chasing financial independence isn't merely a quest for personal wealth; it's a grand symphony where your resources and influence compose a melody of positive change for the world. Imagine your legacy as a masterpiece, a timeless painting of purpose that transcends the boundaries of your lifetime, leaving an indelible mark on the canvas of existence. It's not just about accumulating riches; it's about crafting a narrative of impact and purpose that resonates through the ages.

"The best way to predict the future is to create it."

– Peter Drucker

How can defining your personal values and beliefs guide your philanthropic endeavors?

Defining Embarking on the journey of philanthropy is like navigating the stars guided by your unique constellation of values and beliefs. It's not just about giving; it's about creating a cosmic impact that resonates with your inner compass. Here's your constellation guide:

1. **Celestial Causes:** Picture your values as constellations, guiding you toward causes that twinkle in alignment with your deepest convictions. Your philanthropy becomes a celestial dance, gracefully supporting the issues that truly resonate with your heart.

2. **Navigating the Galactic Opportunities:** Imagine your philanthropic journey as a cosmic expedition, where each decision is a star to be explored. With your values as the cosmic map, you can navigate the vast galaxy of opportunities, ensuring your resources align with the constellations of impact you wish to create.

3. **Constellation of Commitment:** Your values act as the gravity holding your philanthropic constellations together. They form a cosmic force field, keeping you committed and orbiting around your philanthropic goals, no matter the cosmic challenges.

4. Galactic Fulfillment: Aligning your philanthropy with your values is like discovering a new celestial body – it brings a sense of awe and fulfillment. Your contributions become a cosmic masterpiece, painting the universe with the hues of purpose and satisfaction.

So, as you venture into the philanthropic cosmos, let your values be your guiding stars, lighting up the universe with the brilliance of your impact.

Your personal values serve as a guiding light in your philanthropic journey. By understanding and aligning your giving with your core beliefs, you can make a more meaningful and impactful contribution to the causes you care about.

"Living a life of purpose gives you a sense of direction and meaning that is unmatched by any material possession."

– Roy T. Bennett

How can you effectively identify and support organizations that align with your philanthropic goals?

Embarking on the quest to find the perfect philanthropic partner is like uncovering hidden gems in a treasure hunt for meaningful impact. Here's a whimsical guide to navigating this enchanted forest of charitable choices:

1. Research Expedition: Imagine donning an explorer's hat as you embark on a research expedition. Your quest involves delving deep into the lore of potential partners, examining their mission like a treasure map, deciphering their financial transparency as hidden clues, and assessing their overall effectiveness as magical enchantments.

2. Seek Wisened Counsel: Picture yourself in a grand hall of wisdom, seeking counsel from venerable sages of philanthropy. Networking becomes your magical key, unlocking doors to recommendations and insights from those who have traversed these charitable realms before.

3. The Enchanted Encounter: Envision a magical portal that transports you to the heart of philanthropic organizations. As you engage with them directly, attending events and mingling with their enchanted staff and volunteers, you unveil the layers of their mystical work and forge connections that resonate with your values.

4. Heartstrings Connection: Feel the tug of heartstrings as you assess your personal connection to these organizations. It's like discovering a hidden passageway that leads to deeper engagement and satisfaction, where the resonance of shared missions creates a harmonious symphony.

5. Impact Alchemy: Assessing an organization's impact is akin to practicing alchemy, turning data into gold. Delve into their track record, unveil measurable outcomes as mystical potions, and evaluate their ability to weave a lasting spell in the areas that stir your philanthropic soul.

So, as you embark on this fantastical philanthropic journey, may your compass be guided by the spirit of curiosity, your decisions be sprinkled with the dust of wisdom, and your impact be nothing short of magical.

Making informed decisions about your philanthropic contributions requires careful research, due diligence, and a deep understanding of the organizations you support. By identifying and supporting organizations that align with your values and goals, you can maximize your impact and create a lasting positive difference.

"Philanthropy is not about giving away money; it's about giving away your time, your heart, and your soul."

– Richard Carlson

How can you balance your financial goals and aspirations with your philanthropic endeavors?

Embarking on the delicate dance between financial goals and philanthropic aspirations is akin to orchestrating a symphony of purpose and pragmatism. Picture yourself as the conductor, guiding the ensemble through the following harmonious movements:

1. **Financial Sonata:** Envision crafting a musical masterpiece of financial goals, each note representing a defined objective. Setting clear financial goals is akin to composing a sonata, ensuring that the rhythm of your philanthropy harmonizes seamlessly with the melody of your overall financial stability and future plans.

2. **Philanthropic Crescendo:** Picture your budget as the musical score, with philanthropy receiving its dedicated section. Like a crescendo building in intensity, create a philanthropic budget that resonates with your

financial situation, allowing your giving to swell with impact.

3. Melody of Prioritization: Imagine your philanthropy as a musical composition, with each cause as a distinctive melody. Prioritize causes that strike a chord within you, allowing the music of your giving to echo your deepest values. Diversifying your giving is like weaving a rich tapestry of melodies, ensuring your impact is felt across different areas.

4. Responsible Overture: Picture your responsible giving as the opening overture, setting the tone for the entire symphony. Ensure that your philanthropic contributions are made with the precision of a skilled musician, resonating with ethical considerations and a commitment to positive change.

As you stand at the conductor's podium of financial and philanthropic harmony, may your composition be a masterpiece, echoing the resonance of purpose and responsible stewardship.

What are some creative ways to make a positive impact beyond traditional monetary donations?

Venturing beyond the conventional realm of monetary contributions opens up a kaleidoscope of imaginative avenues to weave a tapestry of positive change. Picture yourself as the artisan of impact, sculpting these creative forms of benevolence:

1. Symphony of Time and Talent: Envision volunteering as a virtuoso performance, where your time, skills, and expertise resonate with the mission of organizations. Your contribution becomes a unique melody in the symphony of giving.

2. Gift of Tangibles: Picture your donations of goods and materials as vibrant brushstrokes on a canvas, adding color and substance to the needs of organizations. Whether it's clothing, books, or essential items, your generosity paints a picture of tangible impact.

3. Social Media Advocacy Ballet: Imagine your social media platforms as a stage for a ballet of awareness. With each post and share, you choreograph a dance that enlightens, raises awareness, and advocates for meaningful causes, turning the spotlight on issues that need attention.

4. Mentorship Mosaic: Picture mentorship as a mosaic, where your guidance and support form intricate patterns in the lives of those seeking empowerment. Your role as a mentor adds depth and meaning to the personal and professional journeys of others.

5. Fundraising Symphony: Envision organizing fundraising events as a symphony, where each note represents a community coming together. Your initiatives orchestrate a harmonious blend of awareness, engagement, and financial support for causes close to your heart.

As you embark on this artistic journey of philanthropy, may your creative expressions of generosity paint a canvas of positive change that reverberates far and wide.

Unleashing a positive impact transcends the confines of monetary donations. Picture yourself as a virtuoso orchestrator, weaving a tapestry of change through the threads of your time, skills, influence, and boundless creative ideas. In this symphony of generosity, your contributions become the notes that compose a meaningful melody, echoing through the world and crafting a legacy that extends far beyond the realm of finances.

"The best way to find yourself is to lose yourself in the service of others."

– Mahatma Gandhi

How can you inspire and empower others to pursue their own philanthropic endeavors?

Unleashing the spirit of philanthropy involves more than financial contributions. It's about creating a movement, a ripple effect of generosity that inspires and empowers others. Here's your guide to igniting the flame of giving:

1. Sharing Your Philanthropic Tale: Imagine your philanthropic journey as a captivating storybook, ready to be shared. Open its pages and let the world glimpse into your experiences, motivations, and the profound impact your giving has made. By narrating your story, you become the storyteller who sparks the inspiration for others to embark on their own giving adventures.

2. Mentoring the Philanthropic Novice: Picture yourself as a seasoned guide in the realm of philanthropy. Extend a helping hand to those eager to step into the world of giving. Offer guidance, encouragement, and mentorship to the budding philanthropists, nurturing their passion and helping them navigate the intricate paths of making a difference.

3. Spotlighting the Triumphs of Giving: Envision your philanthropy as a blockbuster film, complete with tales of triumphs and heartwarming narratives. Share these stories with the world. Paint a vivid picture of how giving has transformed lives and communities. Through these cinematic showcases, you become the director, highlighting the positive impact of philanthropy and showcasing its transformative power.

4. Fanning the Flames of Volunteerism: Think of volunteerism as a vibrant garden, ready to bloom with positive change. Urge others to join in the cultivation. Advocate for volunteer opportunities and community engagement, encouraging a culture of giving and social responsibility. In this garden, you're the cultivator, sowing the seeds of altruism and watching the collective impact flourish.

5. Weaving a Tapestry of Philanthropic Allies: Imagine your philanthropic endeavors as threads woven into a rich tapestry. Connect with kindred spirits who share your passion for making a positive impact. Create a supportive network of philanthropists where ideas flow freely, inspirations are exchanged, and a community is formed—one that empowers each member to amplify their philanthropic influence.

In this symphony of giving, you're not just a participant; you're the conductor orchestrating a harmonious melody of inspiration and empowerment.

Igniting the flame of philanthropy is akin to being a beacon, guiding others toward a path of positive change. Imagine yourself as a storyteller, weaving tales of your philanthropic journey that captivate and inspire. Picture extending a helping hand to others, mentoring them as they embark on their own giving adventures. Envision your advocacy for the transformative power of giving as a compelling narrative, encouraging others to join the movement. In this symphony of altruism, you're not just a participant; you're the conductor orchestrating a harmonious melody of inspiration and empowerment.

"A single act of kindness throws a stone into a pond that creates ripples with no end."

– Scott Adams

What are some ways to measure the impact of your philanthropic endeavors?

Delving into the depths of measuring the impact of your philanthropic endeavors unveils a multifaceted approach that goes beyond conventional assessments. Imagine you're not just scrutinizing outcomes but navigating a rich tapestry of effects:

1. Track Tangible Outcomes:

Envision yourself as a meticulous archivist, not merely tracking numbers but narrating stories of lives touched. Each statistic becomes a chapter, revealing the profound impact your support has on individuals, communities, and the world at large.

2. Seek Feedback and Evaluation:

Picture yourself as an empathetic interviewer, seeking insights not just for evaluation but for a shared understanding. The feedback you gather isn't just data; it's a dialogue that nurtures growth and refines the symphony of positive change.

3. Assess Your Own Involvement and Satisfaction:

Imagine a reflective journey where you're not just an observer but an active participant in the canvas of philanthropy. Each reflection is a stroke of self-awareness, painting a picture of your personal engagement and deriving satisfaction from the impact you make.

4. Consider Long-Term Impact:

Envision yourself as a visionary, transcending the immediate horizon to gaze upon a landscape shaped by sustained change. Your philanthropy isn't just a short story; it's an epic, contributing to a legacy of lasting impact and transformative solutions.

5. Seek Expert Guidance:

Picture yourself as a seeker of wisdom, consulting experts not as a mere formality but as a genuine quest for improvement. The guidance you seek isn't just a consultation; it's a collaborative journey toward greater effectiveness in your philanthropic endeavors.

In this exploration, each point isn't a mere step but a vivid scene in the narrative of measuring impact—a tale where your generosity intertwines with the stories of those you aim to uplift.

Navigating the realm of measuring philanthropic impact isn't a mere numerical exercise; it's an odyssey into the heart of real-world change. Imagine it as more than a ledger of statistics but a narrative where tracking outcomes is akin to discovering the plot twists of lives touched. Seeking feedback transforms into a dialogue, not just for evaluation but for a shared understanding that nurtures growth. Reflecting on your involvement becomes a journey of self-discovery, where each moment of engagement is a brushstroke on the canvas of positive change. In this exploration, impact measurement transcends numbers, evolving into a profound understanding of the difference you're crafting in the world.

"To achieve something significant, aim for a target that is beyond you. Do this, and you will grow as you reach for your goal."

– Norman Vincent Peale

How can you effectively communicate your philanthropic endeavors to others?

The journey of communicating your philanthropy isn't just relaying information; it's crafting a narrative that resonates with hearts and minds. Imagine it as an invitation for others to join a movement, where the sharing of your philanthropic journey becomes an inspiration, igniting the spark for change. Transparency and accountability transform into the pillars of a trustworthy legacy, where openness about your giving practices cultivates a culture of responsibility. Picture your philanthropy as a beacon, attracting not just partners but kindred spirits, organizations, or foundations drawn to the shared vision for positive impact. Communicating your goals and strategies becomes a strategic overture, a call that echoes in the hearts of those aligned with your mission. Education takes center stage, with your voice becoming a catalyst for awareness, encouraging others to delve into important causes and spark their journey of understanding. Finally, envision your open discussions not just as a dialogue but as a celebration of giving, fostering a culture where philanthropy is not a choice but a shared ethos.

1. Inspire and Motivate Others:

Imagine your philanthropic journey as a captivating story, narrated with passion and purpose. Share not just the successes but the challenges overcome, turning your experiences into a source of inspiration. Make it personal, allowing others to connect emotionally with the impact you're creating. Your journey should be a beacon, guiding others towards their own philanthropic aspirations.

2. Increase Transparency and Accountability:

Transparency is more than just a buzzword; it's the cornerstone of trust. Paint a vivid picture of your giving practices, showcasing the thought process behind your choices. Make it a journey, where every decision is accounted for and explained. This transforms your communication into a testament of accountability, reinforcing your commitment to responsible philanthropy.

3. Attract Potential Partners and Supporters:

Your communication should be a magnetic force, attracting those who resonate with your mission. Craft a narrative that not only outlines your goals but also invites others to be part of something meaningful. Showcase the collaborative nature of your efforts, turning your philanthropy into a collective endeavor where partners and supporters are integral to the shared vision.

4. Educate Others about Important Causes:

Picture your communication as an enlightening conversation, where each word is a brushstroke painting a vivid image of the causes you support. Go beyond surface-level information; delve into the nuances, complexities, and urgency of the issues. Your communication should be a call to action, urging others to learn, understand, and actively engage with the critical causes you champion.

5. Promote a Culture of Giving:

Envision your communication as the anthem of a cultural shift. Talk not just about your philanthropy but about the broader concept of giving. Normalize the discussion around philanthropy, making it an integral part of everyday conversations. Your voice becomes the catalyst for a culture where generosity is celebrated, and giving back is considered a fundamental aspect of a purposeful life.

In the realm of philanthropy, effective communication is not merely a tool but a superpower that propels the impact of your giving to new heights. Imagine your communication as a well-crafted narrative, where each word is a brushstroke painting a vivid picture of your journey. Don't just share your story; unleash it with passion, making the impact of your giving leap off the page. Engage with others not as an orator but as a storyteller, weaving a tale that inspires, motivates, and educates. In doing so, you become the maestro orchestrating a symphony of positive change that resonates far beyond the realms of your individual efforts.

"The best way to make a difference in the world is to give back and help others."

– Roy T. Bennett

How can you ensure that your philanthropic legacy extends beyond your lifetime?

Ensuring that your philanthropic legacy extends beyond your lifetime requires:

1. Planning and Strategizing Your Giving:

- Dive into the exciting world of long-term philanthropy, where your goals become the stars guiding your unique journey. Picture your strategy as a treasure map leading to a legacy that transcends time and leaves an indelible mark.
- Craft a dynamic roadmap, not just for today's impact but as a time capsule, ensuring your giving adapts and thrives amidst the ever-changing landscape of societal needs.

- Explore imaginative approaches that turn your philanthropy into a living, breathing force, evolving and responding to the world's challenges in real-time.

2. **Establishing a Philanthropic Foundation or Trust:**
   - Imagine your philanthropic foundation or trust as more than a financial entity – see it as the superhero cape that carries your values forward. Design it not just for management but as the guardian of your legacy.
   - Sketch out a blueprint that turns the foundation into a dynamic force, echoing your philanthropic aspirations. Consider seeking the guidance of legal and financial wizards to navigate the magic of setting up a lasting philanthropic institution.
3. **Involving Family and Loved Ones in Your Philanthropy:**
   - Share the enchanting tales behind your philanthropic journey with your family, turning it into a legacy of stories, values, and shared dreams. Make it a narrative that binds generations together.
   - Create a magical space for open discussions, inviting your loved ones to contribute their unique perspectives. Explore collaborative giving projects that feel like a family adventure, fostering a sense of shared purpose and connection.
4. **Supporting Organizations with a Strong Track Record and Succession Planning:**

- Embark on a quest to discover organizations with a proven track record, each one a knight in shining armor making a lasting impact. Picture your support as a beacon that ensures these knights endure and thrive through seamless leadership transitions.
- Seek out partnerships that not only align with your current values but possess the resilience to stand the test of time. Picture these partnerships as timeless alliances, weathering storms and emerging stronger on the other side.

5. Creating a Legacy Statement or Plan:

- Imagine crafting a narrative that goes beyond mere documentation; see it as a spellbinding tale that captures the essence of your philanthropic vision. Turn it into a storybook that guides future decision-makers on an epic journey.
- Weave your values, dreams, and aspirations into a comprehensive legacy statement, creating a narrative that feels like a timeless guide for the next generation of philanthropic dreamweavers. Seek the wisdom of trusted advisors and family members to add diverse threads to this rich tapestry of your philanthropic legacy.

Unleash the magic of your philanthropic legacy, transforming it into a timeless tale that echoes through the corridors of the future. Picture your strategies not as mere plans but as enchanted scrolls, unfurling a narrative that transcends the limits of time. Engage your loved ones as co-authors in this epic story, inviting them to contribute their unique chapters and ensuring your legacy becomes a family saga.

Support organizations not just as beneficiaries of your goodwill but as guardians of your legacy, envisioning them as knights entrusted with the timeless duty of making a lasting impact. Imagine your legacy statement not as a mere document but as a captivating script, a treasure map guiding future explorers through the vast landscapes of your philanthropic dreams. With these elements, your philanthropic legacy becomes a beacon, casting a radiant light that endures, inspiring generations to weave their own chapters into the ever-expanding tapestry of positive change.

"The best legacy is not the wealth we leave behind, but the impact we have on the lives of others."

– Tommy Newberry

10

YOUR JOURNEY BEGINS

Brace yourself for an exhilarating ride as we dive into the heart of your transformative journey. Unlock the potential within you to break free from the chains of financial constraints and step boldly into a future bursting with purpose, passion, and unbridled financial independence. This chapter isn't just a guide; it's a roadmap to action, a blueprint for crafting your own manifesto, and the spark that sets the youth revolution ablaze. Get ready to seize the reins of your destiny and embark on a thrilling adventure toward a life you've always dreamed of.

How can you overcome procrastination and take action towards your financial goals?

Breaking free from the chains of procrastination and taking charge of your financial destiny isn't just a task – it's an adventure waiting to unfold. Let's spice things up and make your journey sizzle with these game-changing strategies:

Embarking on the epic quest towards financial independence is like stepping into a realm of endless possibilities. It's not just a journey; it's a grand adventure waiting to unfold. Buckle up as we transform the mundane act of breaking free from procrastination into a thrilling saga:

Picture this: Your first step is like stepping onto a portal of financial wonders. Setting clear goals isn't just about targets; it's about creating your roadmap to a treasure trove of financial triumphs.

Next up, we're crafting a masterplan – not just any plan, but a detailed, intricate map filled with twists and turns. It's the blueprint to your financial kingdom.

Now, let's talk about scheduling action steps. Imagine it as choreographing a dance routine, but instead of dance moves, it's your daily steps towards financial glory. Make it a routine worth remembering.

Feeling like a lone hero on this quest? Fear not. Your accountability partner or mentor is your trusty sidekick, your guiding star in the financial galaxy.

And finally, reward yourself for progress. Every win, big or small, deserves a celebration. Imagine it as fireworks lighting up your path, marking your journey towards financial brilliance.

This, my friend, is not just a checklist; it's the prologue to your financial epic. Let the adventure begin!

The journey towards financial independence begins with taking that first step, transforming procrastination into action. By setting clear goals, creating a detailed plan, scheduling action steps, finding an accountability partner, and rewarding yourself for progress, you can overcome inertia and propel yourself towards your financial aspirations.

"The journey of a thousand miles begins with a single step."

– Lao Tzu

How can you craft a personal manifesto that encapsulates your financial goals, values, and aspirations?

Crafting a personal manifesto that encapsulates your financial goals, values, and aspirations is akin to composing a unique symphony of your dreams. Begin by tuning into the melody of your goals, defining the notes that resonate with your desired lifestyle and future. Let your values take center stage, guiding your decisions with harmonious principles such as financial freedom, security, community, or passion pursuit.

imagine your ideal financial landscape as a vibrant canvas, each stroke detailing the life you envision. With clarity, forge a declaration that is not just words but a powerful anthem, resonating with the rhythm of your ambitions. This manifesto isn't static; it's a living document. Regularly revisit it, like a virtuoso refining their masterpiece, ensuring it evolves with your changing goals and values.

Your personal manifesto is more than words; it's your guiding star in the financial cosmos. Let it inspire, motivate, and propel you towards the symphony of your financial dreams.

"The future belongs to those who believe in the beauty of their dreams."

– Eleanor Roosevelt

How can you balance pursuing your financial goals with living a fulfilling and purposeful life?

Embarking on the journey to financial independence is an admirable quest, yet the melody of a purposeful life plays not only in the currency of wealth but in the richness of experiences. Imagine this symphony:

Set the stage by establishing boundaries, crafting a dance between financial pursuits and personal well-being. Picture the spotlight shifting to vibrant hues as you delve into hobbies and passions, creating a canvas of joy and fulfillment beyond the ledger.

Cultivate a garden of connections, where relationships with family, friends, and loved ones bloom. See yourself as a conductor orchestrating social impact, contributing your time and skills to causes that resonate, painting strokes of positivity on the canvas of the world.

Now, close your eyes for a moment, let the music soften, and breathe in the essence of gratitude. Reflect on the blessings that transcend material wealth, appreciating the present moment. In this harmonic blend of pursuit and fulfillment, you craft a life that is both financially secure and personally enriching.

Balancing the scales between financial goals and a gratifying existence is an art, and you, my friend, are the masterful artist of your own symphony.

"It is not how much we have,
but how much we give that makes life rich."

– Henry Miller

How can you overcome limiting beliefs and negative self-talk that may hinder your financial progress?

Visualize this: your journey towards financial empowerment is like a grand expedition, but lurking in the shadows are dragons of self-doubt and whispers of negativity. Fear not, for you are equipped with a mighty arsenal:

First, unveil the dragons by identifying and challenging the limiting beliefs, unmasking them for what they truly are. Then, wield the sword of positivity, replacing those self-defeating thoughts with affirmations that resonate with the hero within.

Imagine forging alliances with a fellowship of positivity, surrounding yourself with those who champion your cause. Together, you celebrate victories, no matter how small, fortifying your castle against the onslaught of doubt.

But in the face of relentless shadows, you have the wisdom to seek guidance from mentors, the wizards of the financial realm. They stand ready to assist, armed with spells to dispel the darkest clouds.

In this epic saga, where limiting beliefs are formidable foes, your resilience, affirmations, supportive allies, celebratory rituals, and the wisdom of financial wizards combine to vanquish the shadows. Your financial odyssey unfolds not as a mere conquest but as a heroic tale of triumph over the forces that sought to hinder your progress.

"Whether you think you can or you think you can't, you're right."

– Henry Ford

How can you leverage technology and innovation to enhance your financial success?

Embark on a digital adventure in the realm of financial success, where technology is your trusty sidekick, and innovation is the name of the game. Picture this journey as a thrilling saga, where futuristic tools are your secret weapons, waiting to be unleashed:

Imagine wielding financial apps and tools like a digital superhero, effortlessly managing budgets and making investment decisions with the swipe of a finger. You're not just a budget-savvy individual; you're a tech-savvy maestro orchestrating a symphony of financial prowess.

Now, envision yourself as a digital nomad, navigating the vast landscape of financial trends with ease. Stay ahead of the game by tuning into podcasts, blogs, and news sources that keep you in the loop, transforming financial news into your personalized soundtrack.

Shift gears and become a virtual scholar, delving into the captivating world of online learning platforms. Picture yourself as a knowledge seeker, unlocking the secrets of financial wisdom through webinars and courses that feel more like thrilling episodes than lectures.

In this high-tech escapade, you're not just an investor; you're a trailblazer exploring the frontiers of emerging technologies. Visualize yourself as a pioneer, making strategic moves in the realms of blockchain, artificial intelligence, and fintech, like a digital explorer mapping uncharted territories.

Your financial journey is not a dull expedition; it's a digital quest filled with excitement and futuristic marvels. With financial apps, virtual classrooms, online communities, and cutting-edge investments, you're not just navigating the digital landscape – you're conquering it with flair.

"Technology is not a replacement for human judgment; it complements it."

– Henry Kissinger

How can you cultivate a mindset of abundance and resilience in the face of setbacks and challenges?

Navigating the unpredictable terrain of your financial journey demands a mindset steeped in abundance and resilience. Here are strategies to infuse your mindset with these empowering qualities:

1. **Champion Your Wins:** Take a moment to bask in the glow of your financial victories, no matter how modest. Acknowledging your progress is like shining a spotlight on the positive aspects of your journey.

2. **Challenges as Stepping Stones:** Consider setbacks as brief pauses in the melody of your financial journey, opportunities for learning and growth. Believe in your ability to dance through challenges, emerging wiser and more resilient.

3. Daily Gratitude Rituals: Cultivate a habit of expressing gratitude, recognizing both financial and non-financial blessings. This daily ritual becomes a powerful tonic, fostering contentment and genuine appreciation.

4. Positivity in Your Circle: Surround yourself with the cheerleaders, the ones who not only believe in your potential but also inspire you to persevere. Their positivity becomes a shield during tough times.

5. Nurture a Growth Mindset: Embrace challenges not as roadblocks but as avenues for growth and learning. Foster the belief that your abilities are dynamic, capable of flourishing with dedication and effort.

By weaving these strategies into the fabric of your mindset, you don't just navigate setbacks; you transform them into stepping stones that propel you forward. Your journey becomes a canvas where positivity, gratitude, and resilience paint the picture of your enduring financial success.

"The only thing that makes life possible is permanent, intolerable uncertainty: not knowing what comes next."

– Ursula K. Le Guin

How can you build a strong financial foundation and protect your financial well-being?

The financial journey is like setting sail on an adventure, and a mindset of abundance and resilience is your compass guiding you through the twists and turns. Imagine this mindset as a powerful force, shaping your narrative in the most empowering way:

imagine yourself on the deck of your financial ship, basking in the glow of positivity. Instead of focusing on stormy seas, acknowledge the progress you've made, the achievements that sparkle like stars, and the treasure trove of resources at your disposal. You're not just a sailor; you're the captain of your financial destiny, navigating by the light of your accomplishments.

As you encounter setbacks, visualize them as temporary detours in your grand expedition. Believe in your ability to weather the storms, learn from the challenges, and bounce back with renewed vigor. These setbacks are not roadblocks; they're the thrilling plot twists that make your financial saga all the more compelling.

Now, imagine practicing gratitude as your secret weapon. Express gratitude for the financial and non-financial blessings in your life, creating a shield of contentment and appreciation. It's not just an attitude; it's a superpower that keeps your spirit resilient in the face of financial tempests.

Surround yourself with a crew of positive and supportive individuals who inspire, believe in your potential, and cheer you on. You're not sailing alone; you're part of a fellowship that shares the vision of financial success and encourages you to persevere, making the journey more joyful and rewarding.

Embrace a growth mindset as the wind in your sails, propelling you forward. View challenges not as obstacles, but as opportunities for growth and learning. Your abilities are not fixed; they're sails that can be adjusted and strengthened through dedication and effort. In this mindset, setbacks become stepping stones, and resilience becomes the wind that propels you towards your financial goals.

"A fool and his money are soon parted."

– Benjamin Franklin

How can you contribute to a more equitable and sustainable financial future for all?

The road to financial independence is not just a solo expedition; it's a chance to become a pioneer of positive change in the financial landscape. Envision your journey as a transformative force, where your actions contribute to a future that's not just about personal success but shared prosperity:

Imagine yourself as a torchbearer, illuminating the path for others through support for financial literacy initiatives. You're not just learning for yourself; you're advocating for programs that empower underserved communities with the knowledge to make informed financial decisions. Your journey becomes a beacon of enlightenment, breaking down barriers to financial understanding.

Now, picture your investments as seeds sown in a field of ethical and sustainable practices. Allocate a portion to companies that prioritize not just profits but ethical standards, environmental sustainability, and social responsibility. Your investment portfolio becomes a garden, cultivating a financial future where ethical business practices bloom.

Consider your involvement with organizations promoting financial inclusion as the bridge to a more equitable world. You're not merely a spectator; you're an advocate and supporter, ensuring that access to financial services, from microloans to counseling, reaches marginalized communities. Your journey becomes a bridge, connecting individuals to the financial resources they deserve.

Envision your lifestyle choices as ripples in a pond of responsible consumerism. Promote conscious consumption habits and sustainable practices, creating a ripple effect that reduces environmental impact and supports businesses with ethical values. Your journey becomes a ripple, creating waves of change in the way we consume and interact with the financial world.

Now, imagine yourself as a storyteller, sharing your financial knowledge and experiences to raise awareness. It's not just about your personal journey; it's about educating others on financial literacy, responsible investing, and the importance of inclusion. Your journey becomes a narrative, inspiring others to join the movement towards a financial future that is accessible and sustainable for all.

"The ultimate measure of a man is not where he stands in moments of comfort and convenience, but where he stands at times of challenge and controversy."

– Martin Luther King, Jr.

How can you overcome the fear of failure and embrace the spirit of risk-taking in your financial endeavors?

In the realm of financial pursuits, the fear of failure often lurks like a shadow, casting doubt on the path to progress. But imagine this fear not as a stop sign but as a crossroads where calculated risk-taking becomes your compass. Let's unravel the strategies that transform fear into a catalyst for financial growth:

Visualize failure as a wise teacher, not a stern judge. See setbacks as stepping stones, not stumbling blocks. Reframe failure as a canvas where each mistake paints a lesson, contributing strokes to the masterpiece of your financial journey. Your fear transforms into a guide, pushing you towards the vast landscape of learning opportunities.

Now, envision yourself as a scholar of risk management, decoding the language of uncertainties. Educate yourself on the principles and techniques that navigate the labyrinth of risks. Your journey becomes a classroom, where each lesson equips you with the tools to make informed decisions, shielding your ambitions from the potential storms of failure.

Start your financial odyssey on the shores of caution, dipping your toes in low-risk investments. Picture each venture as a stepping stone, a staircase leading to the balcony of confidence. As you ascend, your risk tolerance expands like a blooming flower, fueled by the sunlight of experience.

Now, imagine experienced mentors as lighthouses guiding your financial ship through treacherous waters. Seek their wisdom, bask in their light, and let their insights navigate your journey. Your fears dissolve in the illumination of shared experiences, and your path becomes clearer with each conversation.

Finally, embrace calculated risk-taking as the heartbeat of innovation. Picture it not as a leap into the unknown but as a dance with opportunity. Your journey becomes a stage, where each calculated risk is a choreographed move towards growth, a rhythm that resonates with the pursuit of your financial dreams. Fear transforms into a mere background note, drowned out by the melody of potential success.

"The greatest glory in living lies not in never falling, but in rising every time we fall."

– Nelson Mandela

How can you maintain a healthy and balanced lifestyle while pursuing your financial goals?

In the grand symphony of life, the pursuit of financial success is but one note, harmonizing with the broader melody of overall well-being. Imagine this journey not as a sprint to the finish line but as a leisurely stroll through the garden of fulfillment, where each step is savored. Let's explore the strategies that weave the threads of financial aspirations into the tapestry of a healthy and balanced lifestyle:

Visualize your physical health as the cornerstone, a sturdy pillar that supports the structure of your financial endeavors. Engage in a rhythmic dance with regular exercise, nourish your body with a palette of nutritious foods, and let the curtains fall gracefully for a restful night's sleep. Picture these habits as the secret ingredients, infusing your journey with the energy, focus, and resilience needed to navigate the financial landscape.

Now, envision mental well-being as the artist's palette, an array of colors that paint the canvas of your financial decisions. Practice mindfulness as strokes of serenity, engage in activities that spark joy as vibrant hues, and reach out to loved ones or professionals as the skilled hands that mold your emotional clay. This canvas, painted with positivity and emotional well-being, becomes the masterpiece that guides your financial brushstrokes.

Cultivate strong social connections as the supporting cast in your life's play. Imagine meaningful relationships as the plot twists, providing a sense of belonging, support, and a network that enriches your narrative beyond financial achievements. Picture these connections as the backdrop, enhancing the overall storyline of your life.

Schedule time for personal pursuits as the interlude between financial chapters. Dedicate moments to hobbies, interests, and activities that bring you joy, offering a refreshing breeze amid the complexities of financial endeavors. These personal pursuits become the soothing rhythm, providing an outlet for relaxation, creativity, and personal growth.

Should the intricacies of your financial journey ever cast shadows on your overall well-being, consider seeking guidance from the conductors of life — therapists, counselors, or life coaches. Picture them as the maestros, guiding you through the symphony of self-discovery, helping you strike a harmonious balance between financial aspirations and the orchestra of your well-being.

Remember, the pursuit of financial success is not a race against time; it's a leisurely waltz to be enjoyed. By prioritizing physical, mental, and social well-being, you compose a life where financial success complements, rather than overshadows, your overall happiness and fulfillment.

"True wealth is not in the abundance of possessions, but in the richness of experiences."

– H. Jackson Brown, Jr.

How can you harness the power of gratitude and cultivate a spirit of abundance to transform your financial future and achieve your ultimate financial goals?

the thrilling journey to financial independence is like strapping into a roller coaster of possibilities, with loops of gratitude and drops of abundance awaiting you. Imagine being the G person destined for greatness, navigating twists and turns with unshakeable confidence. Now, let's ditch the textbooks and dive into a storytelling adventure where gratitude and abundance become your trusty sidekicks in this epic financial saga.

Embrace Gratitude: The Magic Wand of Abundance

Picture gratitude as your magical lens, not just any lens but one that transforms your view from "I wish" to "look what I've got!" It's like upgrading your vision to see opportunities sprouting where limitations used to cast shadows. Ready to put on those gratitude glasses?

Cultivate Abundance: Unlocking Your Inner Money Magician

Now, let's talk abundance – the secret sauce that turns your financial dreams from 'maybe' to 'definitely.' It's like having your own money magic wand, where you don't just see wealth as a far-off castle but as your cozy home. And guess what? Your positive thinking is the enchantment that opens the door to a land of endless possibilities.

Transforming Your Financial Future: Gratitude and Abundance as Your Superpowers

So, how do you infuse this magic into your financial journey? Get ready for some enchanting practices:

Daily Gratitude Quest: Think of this as your daily treasure hunt. Seek out the financial and non-financial treasures in your life and revel in them. It's like finding hidden gems and shouting, "Eureka!"

Celebrate Your Wins: Every financial milestone, big or small, deserves a celebration. Imagine each win as a level-up in your financial video game – cue the confetti!

Focus on Your Treasure Trove: Turn away from the 'wish I had' to 'look at all this cool stuff.' Your financial landscape is a treasure trove waiting to be explored. Ready to uncover the richness?

Visualize Your Financial Fairy Tale: Close your eyes and picture your dream financial scenario. It's not just a vision board; it's your own financial fairy tale where you're the hero or heroine.

Share Your Financial Adventures: Ever heard the saying, "Sharing is caring"? Spread the magic by telling others about your financial escapades. You're not bragging; you're inspiring!

Sprinkle Goodness Around: Remember the magic wand? Now it's time to use it for good. Support causes close to your heart and watch the ripple effect of goodness.

Now, imagine your financial journey as a thrilling adventure novel. Gratitude and abundance are the plot twists that keep you turning the pages, eager to find out what happens next. Embrace the magic, and let the enchantment of gratitude and abundance propel you towards becoming the top G person you were born to be. Get ready for a journey where financial wisdom meets whimsy, and the only textbook is the story you're living.

"We are the masters of our fate.
We are the captains of our souls."

– Winston Churchill

Congratulations, Trailblazer!

As you conclude this thrilling journey, remember, you're not just closing a chapter; you're unplugging from the Matrix and breaking free from the relentless race of the conventional. This isn't merely the end of a book; it's the escape route you've discovered from the rat race, a key to unlocking financial freedom in the grandest sense.

As you turn the final page, take a moment to reflect on the chapters you've navigated—the challenges, victories, and the personal growth you've experienced. You are now the author of your financial story, but not just any story—a narrative of liberation from the Matrix and the pursuit of a life unshackled by the ordinary.

The grand finale isn't about the destination; it's about the journey you've undertaken, breaking away from the predefined roles and scripts. You've cultivated a mindset of abundance, harnessed the power of gratitude, and embraced the spirit of financial independence as the means to escape the Matrix.

Now, go out and live the sequel, the trilogy, and beyond, all while staying untethered from the conventional narrative. Whether you're dodging financial agents, outsmarting the system, or envisioning a life beyond the coded reality, remember: You are the Neo of your financial tale.

But here's the secret—you're not alone. The knowledge gained, the habits formed, and the mindset cultivated are your loyal companions on this journey out of the Matrix. As you step into the sequel, carry with you the lessons, the magic, and the unwavering belief in your ability to script the life you desire and escape the rat race.

So, Trailblazer, what's next for you? What new adventures, challenges, and triumphs await in the upcoming chapters outside the Matrix? The beauty lies in the uncertainty, the unwritten pages waiting for your unique story to unfold.

May your financial future be as liberating as the story you've just lived. Here's to a life of abundance, gratitude, and continuous financial growth, all while evading the confines of the Matrix and the clutches of the rat race.

Until the next chapter, Trailblazer. Your escape from the Matrix and financial adventure awaits!

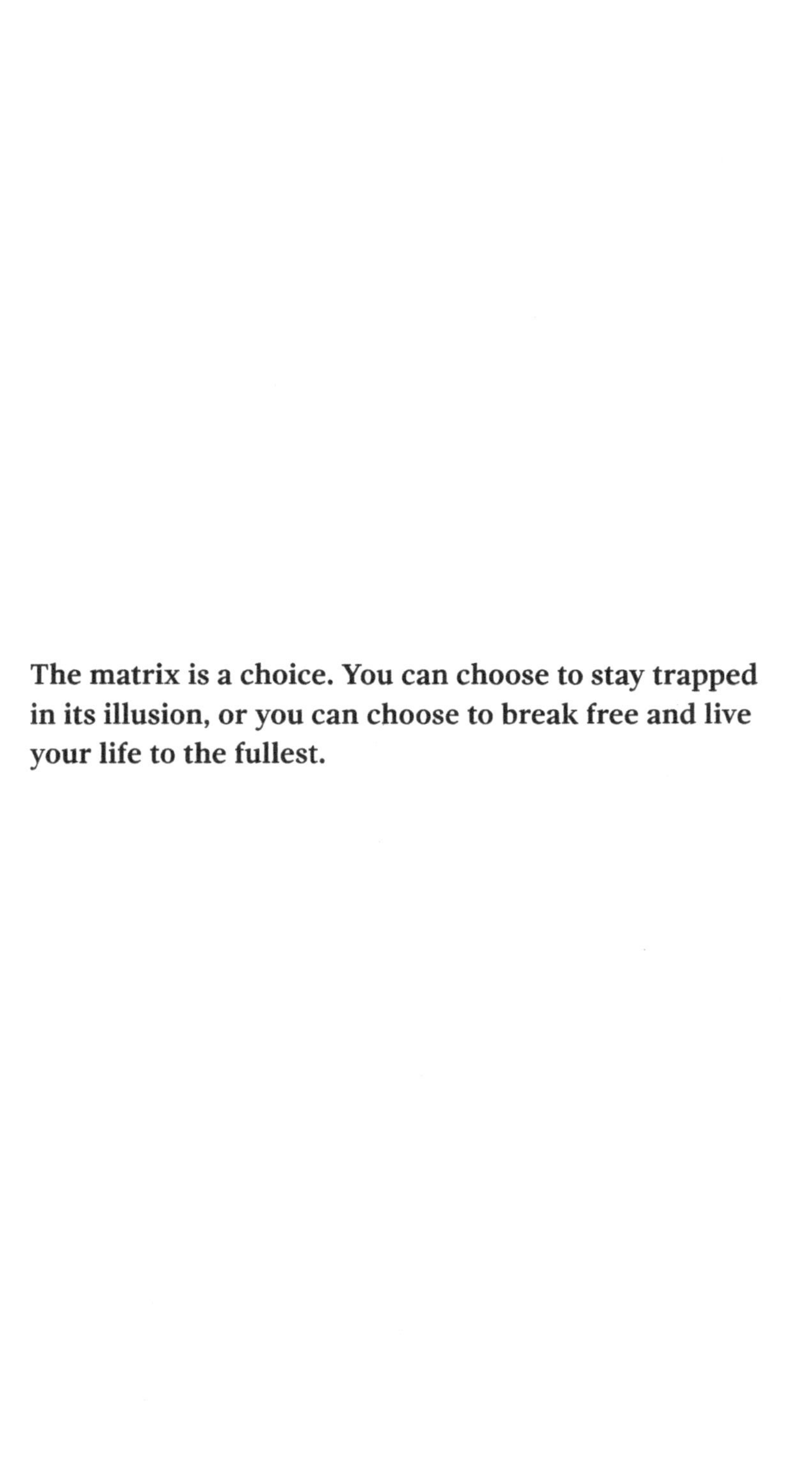

The matrix is a choice. You can choose to stay trapped in its illusion, or you can choose to break free and live your life to the fullest.

www.ingramcontent.com/pod-product-compliance
Lightning Source LLC
LaVergne TN
LVHW041100150826
845673LV00007B/1857

* 9 7 9 8 8 9 4 4 6 0 6 6 6 *